IDENTIFICATION OF STUDENTS FOR GIFTED AND TALENTED PROGRAMS

ESSENTIAL READINGS IN GIFTED EDUCATION

SERIES EDITOR
SALLY M. REIS

Joseph S. Renzulli
EDITOR

IDENTIFICATION OF STUDENTS FOR GIFTED AND TALENTED PROGRAMS

A Joint Publication of Corwin Press and the National Association for Gifted Children

ESSENTIAL READINGS IN GIFTED EDUCATION
Sally M. Reis, SERIES EDITOR

CORWIN PRESS
A Sage Publications Company
Thousand Oaks, California

For information:

Corwin Press
A Sage Publications Company
2455 Teller Road
Thousand Oaks, California 91320
www.corwinpress.com

Sage Publications Ltd
1 Oliver's Yard
55 City Road
London EC1Y 1SP
United Kingdom

Sage Publications India Pvt. Ltd.
B-42, Panchsheel Enclave
Post Box 4109
New Delhi 110 017 India

Printed in the United States of America

Library of Congress Cataloging-in-Publication Data

Identification of students for gifted and talented programs / Joseph S. Renzulli, editor.
    p. cm. — (Essential readings in gifted education ; 2)
"A Joint Publication of Corwin Press and the National Association for Gifted Children."
Includes bibliographical references and index.
ISBN 978-1-4129-0428-5 (pbk.)
    1. Gifted children—Education—United States. 2. Gifted children—United States—
Identification. I. Renzulli, Joseph S. II. National Association for Gifted Children (U.S.) III. Series.
LC3993.9.I53 2004
371.95—dc22

                          2004001000

This book is printed on acid-free paper.

08   10   9   8   7   6   5   4

Acquisitions Editor:	Kylee Liegl
Editorial Assistant:	Jaime Cuvier
Production Editor:	Sanford Robinson
Typesetter:	C&M Digitals (P) Ltd.
Cover Designer:	Tracy E. Miller

NAGC Publications Coordinator: Jane Clarenbach

Contents

About the Editors

Sally M. Reis is a professor and the department head of the Educational Psychology Department at the University of Connecticut where she also serves as principal investigator of the National Research Center on the Gifted and Talented. She was a teacher for 15 years, 11 of which were spent working with gifted students on the elementary, junior high, and high school levels. She has authored more than 130 articles, 9 books, 40 book chapters, and numerous monographs and technical reports.

Her research interests are related to special populations of gifted and talented students, including: students with learning disabilities, gifted females and diverse groups of talented students. She is also interested in extensions of the Schoolwide Enrichment Model for both gifted and talented students and as a way to expand offerings and provide general enrichment to identify talents and potentials in students who have not been previously identified as gifted.

She has traveled extensively conducting workshops and providing professional development for school districts on gifted education, enrichment programs, and talent development programs. She is co-author of *The Schoolwide Enrichment Model, The Secondary Triad Model, Dilemmas in Talent Development in the Middle Years,* and a book published in 1998 about women's talent development titled *Work Left Undone: Choices and Compromises of Talented Females.* Sally serves on several editorial boards, including the *Gifted Child Quarterly,* and is a past president of the National Association for Gifted Children.

Joseph S. Renzulli is Professor of Educational Psychology at the University of Connecticut, where he also serves as director of the National Research Center on the Gifted and Talented. His research has focused on the identification and development of creativity and giftedness in young people and on organizational models and curricular strategies for total school improvement. A focus of his work has been on applying the strategies of gifted education to the improvement of learning for all students. He is a Fellow in the American Psychological Association and was a consultant to the White House Task Force on Education of the Gifted and Talented. He was recently designated a Board of Trustees Distinguished Professor at the University of Connecticut, and in 2003 he was awarded an Honorary Doctor of Law Degree from McGill University in Montreal, Canada. Although he has obtained more than $20 million in research grants, he lists as his proudest professional accomplishments the UConn Mentor Connection program for gifted young students and the summer Confratute program at UConn, which began in 1978 and has served thousands of teachers and administrators from around the world.

Series Introduction

Sally M. Reis

The accomplishments of the last 50 years in the education of gifted students should not be underestimated: the field of education of the gifted and talented has emerged as strong and visible. In many states, a policy or position statement from the state board of education supports the education of the gifted and talented, and specific legislation generally recognizes the special needs of this group. Growth in our field has not been constant, however, and researchers and scholars have discussed the various high and low points of national interest and commitment to educating the gifted and talented (Gallagher, 1979; Renzulli, 1980; Tannenbaum, 1983). Gallagher described the struggle between support and apathy for special programs for gifted and talented students as having roots in historical tradition—the battle between an aristocratic elite and our concomitant belief in egalitarianism. Tannenbaum suggested the existence of two peak periods of interest in the gifted as the five years following *Sputnik* in 1957 and the last half of the decade of the 1970s, describing a valley of neglect between the peaks in which the public focused its attention on the disadvantaged and the handicapped. "The cyclical nature of interest in the gifted is probably unique in American education. No other special group of children has been alternately embraced and repelled with so much vigor by educators and laypersons alike" (Tannenbaum, 1983, p. 16). Many wonder if the cyclical nature to which Tannenbaum referred is not somewhat prophetic, as it appears that our field may be experiencing another downward spiral in interest as a result of current governmental initiatives and an increasing emphasis on testing and standardization of curriculum. Tannenbaum's description of a valley of neglect may describe current conditions. During the late 1980s, programming flourished during a peak of interest and a textbook on systems and models for gifted programs included 15 models for elementary and secondary programs (Renzulli, 1986). The Jacob Javits Gifted and Talented Students Education Act passed by Congress in 1988 resulted in the creation of the National Research Center on the Gifted and Talented, and dozens of model programs were added to the collective knowledge in the field in areas related to underrepresented populations and successful practices. In the 1990s, reduction or elimination of gifted programs occurred, as budget pressures exacerbated by the lingering recession in the late 1990s resulted in the reduction of services mandated by fewer than half of the states in our country.

Even during times in which more activity focused on the needs of gifted and talented students, concerns were still raised about the limited services provided to these students. In the second federal report on the status of education for our nation's most talented students entitled *National Excellence: A Case for Developing America's Talent* (Ross, 1993), "a quiet crisis" was described in the absence of attention paid to this population: "Despite sporadic attention over the years to the needs of bright students, most of them continue to spend time in school working well below their capabilities. The belief espoused in school reform that children from all economic and cultural backgrounds must reach their full potential has not been extended to America's most talented students. They are under-challenged and therefore underachieve" (p. 5). The report further indicates that our nation's gifted and talented students have a less rigorous curriculum, read fewer demanding books, and are less prepared for work or postsecondary education than the most talented students in many other industrialized countries. Talented children who come from economically disadvantaged homes or are members of minority groups are especially neglected, the report also indicates, and many of them will not realize their potential without some type of intervention.

In this anniversary series of volumes celebrating the evolution of our field, noted scholars introduce a collection of the most frequently cited articles from the premiere journal in our field, *Gifted Child Quarterly*. Each volume includes a collection of thoughtful, and in some cases, provocative articles that honor our past, acknowledge the challenges we face in the present, and provide hopeful guidance for the future as we seek the optimal educational experiences for all talented students. These influential articles, published after a rigorous peer review, were selected because they are frequently cited and considered seminal in our field. Considered in their entirety, the articles show that we have learned a great deal from the volume of work represented by this series. Our knowledge has expanded over several decades of work, and progress has been made toward reaching consensus about what is known. As several of the noted scholars who introduce separate areas explain in their introductions, this series helps us to understand that some questions have been answered, while others remain. While we still search for these answers, we are now better prepared to ask questions that continue and evolve. The seminal articles in this series help us to resolve some issues, while they highlight other questions that simply refuse to go away. Finally, the articles help us to identify new challenges that continue to emerge in our field. Carol Tomlinson suggests, for example, that the area of curriculum differentiation in the field of gifted education is, in her words, an issue born in the field of gifted education, and one that continues to experience rebirth.

Some of the earliest questions in our field have been answered and time has enabled those answers to be considered part of our common core of knowledge. For example, it is widely acknowledged that both school and home experiences can help to develop giftedness in persons with high potential and that a continuum of services in and out of school can provide the greatest likelihood that this development will occur. Debates over other "hot" issues such as grouping and acceleration that took place in the gifted education community 30 years ago are now largely unnecessary, as Linda Brody points out in her introduction to a series of articles in this area. General agreement seems to have been reached, for example, that grouping, enrichment and acceleration are all necessary to provide appropriate educational opportunities for gifted and talented learners. These healthy debates of the past helped to strengthen our field but visionary and reflective work remains to be done. In this series, section editors summarize what has been learned and raise provocative questions about the future. The questions alone are some of the most thoughtful in our field, providing enough research opportunities for scholars for the next decade. The brief introductions below provide some highlights about the series.

DEFINITIONS OF GIFTEDNESS (VOLUME 1)

In Volume 1, Robert Sternberg introduces us to seminal articles about definitions of giftedness and the types of talents and gifts exhibited by children and youth. The most widely used definitions of gifts and talents utilized by educators generally follow those proposed in federal reports. For example, the Marland Report (Marland, 1972) commissioned by the Congress included the first federal definition of giftedness, which was widely adopted or adapted by the states.

The selection of a definition of giftedness has been and continues to be the major policy decision made at state and local levels. It is interesting to note that policy decisions are often either unrelated or marginally related to actual procedures or to research findings about a definition of giftedness or identification of the gifted, a fact well documented by the many ineffective, incorrect, and downright ridiculous methods of identification used to find students who meet the criteria in the federal definition. This gap between policy and practice may be caused by many variables. Unfortunately, although the federal definition was written to be inclusive, it is, instead, rather vague, and problems caused by this definition have been recognized by experts in the field (Renzulli, 1978). In the most recent federal report on the status of gifted and talented programs entitled *National Excellence* (Ross, 1993), a newer federal definition is proposed based on new insights provided by neuroscience and cognitive psychology. Arguing that the term *gifted* connotes a mature power rather than a developing ability and, therefore, is antithetic to recent research findings about children, the new definition "reflects today's knowledge and thinking" (p. 26) by emphasizing talent development, stating that gifted and talented children are children and youth with outstanding talent performance or show the potential for performing at remarkably high levels of accomplishment when compared with others of their age, experience, or environment. These children and youth exhibit high performance capability in intellectual, creative, and/or artistic areas, possess an unusual leadership capacity, or excel in specific academic fields. They require services or activities not ordinarily provided by the schools. Outstanding talents are present in children and youth from all cultural groups, across all economic strata, and in all areas of human endeavor. (p. 26)

Fair identification systems use a variety of multiple assessment measures that respect diversity, accommodate students who develop at different rates, and identify potential as well as demonstrated talent. In the introduction to the volume, Sternberg admits, that just as people have bad habits, so do academic fields, explaining, "a bad habit of much of the gifted field is to do research on giftedness, or worse, identify children as gifted or not gifted, without having a clear conception of what it means to be gifted." Sternberg summarizes major themes from the seminal articles about definitions by asking key questions about the nature of giftedness and talent, the ways in which we should study giftedness, whether we should expand conventional notions of giftedness, and if so, how that can be accomplished; whether differences exist between giftedness and talent; the validity of available assessments; and perhaps most importantly, how do we and can we develop giftedness and talent. Sternberg succinctly summarizes points of broad agreement from the many scholars who have contributed to this section, concluding that giftedness involves more than just high IQ, that it has noncognitive and cognitive components, that the environment is crucial in terms of whether potentials for gifted performance will be realized, and that giftedness is not a single thing. He further cautions that the ways we conceptualize giftedness greatly influences who will have opportunities to develop their gifts and reminds readers of our responsibilities as educators. He also asks one of the most critical questions in our field: whether gifted and talented individuals will use their knowledge to benefit or harm our world.

IDENTIFICATION OF HIGH-ABILITY STUDENTS (VOLUME 2)

In Volume 2, Joseph Renzulli introduces what is perhaps the most critical question still facing practitioners and researchers in our field, that is how, when, and why should we identify gifted and talented students. Renzulli believes that conceptions of giftedness exist along a continuum ranging from a very conservative or restricted view of giftedness to a more flexible or multidimensional approach. What many seem not to understand is that the first step in identification should always be to ask: identification for what? For what type of program or experience is the youngster being identified? If, for example, an arts program is being developed for talented artists, the resulting identification system must be structured to identify youngsters with either demonstrated or potential talent in art.

Renzulli's introductory chapter summarizes seminal articles about identification, and summarizes emerging consensus. For example, most suggest, that while intelligence tests and other cognitive ability tests provide one very important form of information about one dimension of a young person's potential, mainly in the areas of verbal and analytic skills, they do not tell us all that we need to know about who should be identified. These authors do not argue that cognitive ability tests should be dropped from the identification process. Rather, most believe that (a) other indicators of potential should be used for identification, (b) these indicators should be given equal consideration when it comes to making final decisions about which students will be candidates for special services, and (c) in the final analysis, it is the thoughtful judgment of knowledgeable professionals rather than instruments and cutoff scores that should guide selection decisions.

Another issue addressed by the authors of the seminal articles about identification is what has been referred to as the distinction between (a) convergent and divergent thinking (Guilford, 1967; Torrance, 1984), (b) entrenchment and non-entrenchment (Sternberg, 1982), and (c) schoolhouse giftedness versus creative/productive giftedness (Renzulli, 1982; Renzulli & Delcourt, 1986). It is easier to identify schoolhouse giftedness than it is to identify students with the potential for creative productive giftedness. Renzulli believes that progress has been made in the identification of gifted students, especially during the past quarter century, and that new approaches address the equity issue, policies, and practices that respect new theories about human potential and conceptions of giftedness. He also believes, however, that continuous commitment to research-based identification practices is still needed, for "it is important to keep in mind that some of the characteristics that have led to the recognition of history's most gifted contributors are not always as measurable as others. We need to continue our search for those elusive things that are left over after everything explainable has been explained, to realize that giftedness is culturally and contextually imbedded in all human activity, and most of all, to value the value of even those things that we cannot yet explain."

ACCELERATION AND GROUPING, CURRICULUM, AND CURRICULUM DIFFERENTIATION (VOLUMES 3, 4, 5)

Three volumes in this series address curricular and grouping issues in gifted programs, and it is in this area, perhaps, that some of the most promising practices have been implemented for gifted and talented students. Grouping and curriculum interact with each other, as various forms of grouping patterns have enabled students to work on advanced curricular opportunities with other talented students. And, as is commonly known now about instructional and ability grouping, it is not the way students are grouped that matters most, but rather, it is what happens within the groups that makes the most difference.

In too many school settings, little differentiation of curriculum and instruction for gifted students is provided during the school day, and minimal opportunities are offered. Occasionally, after-school enrichment programs or Saturday programs offered by museums, science centers, or local universities take the place of comprehensive school programs, and too many academically talented students attend school in classrooms across the country in which they are bored, unmotivated, and unchallenged. Acceleration, once a frequently used educational practice in our country, is often dismissed by teachers and administrators as an inappropriate practice for a variety of reasons, including scheduling problems, concerns about the social effects of grade skipping, and others. Various forms of acceleration, including enabling precocious students to enter kindergarten or first grade early, grade skipping, and early entrance to college are not commonly used by most school districts.

Unfortunately, major alternative grouping strategies involve the reorganization of school structures, and these have been too slow in coming, perhaps due to the difficulty of making major educational changes, because of scheduling, finances, and other issues that have caused schools to substantially delay major change patterns. Because of this delay, gifted students too often fail to receive classroom instruction based on their unique needs that place them far ahead of their chronological peers in basic skills and verbal abilities and enable them to learn much more rapidly and tackle much more complex materials than their peers. Our most able students need appropriately paced, rich and challenging instruction, and curriculum that varies significantly from what is being taught in regular classrooms across America. Too often, academically talented students are "left behind" in school.

Linda Brody introduces the question of how to group students optimally for instructional purposes and pays particular concern to the degree to which the typical age-in-grade instructional program can meet the needs of gifted students—those students with advanced cognitive abilities and achievement that may already have mastered the curriculum designed for their age peers. The articles about grouping emphasize the importance of responding to the learning needs of individual students with curricular flexibility, the need for educators to be flexible when assigning students to instructional groups, and the need to modify those groups when necessary. Brody's introduction points out that the debate about grouping gifted and talented learners together was one area that brought the field together, as every researcher in the field supports some type of grouping option, and few would disagree with the need to use grouping and accelerated learning as tools that allow us to differentiate content for students with different learning needs. When utilized as a way to offer a more advanced educational program to students with advanced cognitive abilities and achievement levels, these practices can help achieve the goal of an appropriate education for all students.

Joyce VanTassel-Baska introduces the seminal articles in curriculum, by explaining that they represent several big ideas that emphasize the values and relevant factors of a curriculum for the gifted, the technology of curriculum development, aspects of differentiation of a curriculum for the gifted within core subject areas and without, and the research-based efficacy of such curriculum and related instructional pedagogy in use. She also reminds readers of Harry Passow's concerns about curriculum balance, suggesting that an imbalance exists, as little evidence suggests that the affective development of gifted students is occurring through special curricula for the gifted. Moreover, interdisciplinary efforts at curriculum frequently exclude the arts and foreign language. Only through acknowledging and applying curriculum balance in these areas are we likely to be producing the type of humane individual Passow envisioned. To achieve balance, VanTassel-Baska recommends a full set of curriculum options across domains, as well as the need to nurture the social-emotional needs of diverse gifted and talented learners.

Carol Tomlinson introduces the critical area of differentiation in the field of gifted education that has only emerged in the last 13 years. She believes the diverse nature of the articles and their relatively recent publication suggests that this area is indeed, in her words, "an issue born in the field of gifted education, and one that continues to experience rebirth." She suggests that one helpful way of thinking about the articles in this volume is that their approach varies, as some approach the topic of differentiation of curriculum with a greater emphasis on the distinctive mission of gifted education. Others look at differentiation with a greater emphasis on the goals, issues, and missions shared between general education and gifted education. Drawing from an analogy with anthropology, Tomlinson suggests that "splitters" in that field focus on differences among cultures while "lumpers" have a greater interest in what cultures share in common. Splitters ask the question of what happens for high-ability students in mixed-ability settings, while lumpers question what common issues and solutions exist for multiple populations in mixed-ability settings.

Tomlinson suggests that the most compelling feature of the collection of articles in this section—and certainly its key unifying feature—is the linkage between the two areas of educational practice in attempting to address an issue likely to be seminal to the success of both over the coming quarter century and beyond, and this collection may serve as a catalyst for next steps in those directions for the field of gifted education as it continues collaboration with general education and other educational specialties while simultaneously addressing those missions uniquely its own.

UNDERREPRESENTED AND TWICE-EXCEPTIONAL POPULATIONS AND SOCIAL AND EMOTIONAL ISSUES (VOLUMES 6, 7, 8)

The majority of young people participating in gifted and talented programs across the country continue to represent the majority culture in our society. Few doubts exist regarding the reasons that economically disadvantaged, twice-exceptional, and culturally diverse students are underrepresented in gifted programs. One reason may be the ineffective and inappropriate identification and selection procedures used for the identification of these young people that limits referrals and nominations and eventual placement. Research summarized in this series indicates that groups that have been traditionally underrepresented in gifted programs could be better served if some of the following elements are considered: new constructs of giftedness, attention to cultural and contextual variability, the use of more varied and authentic assessments, performance-based identification, and identification opportunities through rich and varied learning opportunities.

Alexinia Baldwin discusses the lower participation of culturally diverse and underserved populations in programs for the gifted as a major concern that has forged dialogues and discussion in *Gifted Child Quarterly* over the past five decades. She classifies these concerns in three major themes: *identification/selection*, *programming*, and *staff assignment and development*. Calling the first theme **Identification/Selection**, she indicates that it has always been the Achilles' heel of educators' efforts to ensure that giftedness can be expressed in many ways through broad identification techniques. Citing favorable early work by Renzulli and Hartman (1971) and Baldwin (1977) that expanded options for identification, Baldwin cautions that much remains to be done. The second theme, **Programming**, recognizes the abilities of students who are culturally diverse but often forces them to exist in programs designed "for one size fits all." Her third theme relates to **Staffing and Research**, as she voices concerns about the diversity of teachers in these programs as well as the attitudes or mindsets of researchers who develop theories and conduct the research that addresses these concerns.

Susan Baum traces the historical roots of gifted and talented individuals with special needs, summarizing Terman's early work that suggested the gifted were healthier, more popular, and better adjusted than their less able peers. More importantly, gifted individuals were regarded as those who could perform at high levels in all areas with little or no support. Baum suggests that acceptance of these stereotypical characteristics diminished the possibility that there could be special populations of gifted students with special needs. Baum believes that the seminal articles in this collection address one or more of the critical issues that face gifted students at risk and suggest strategies for overcoming the barriers that prevent them from realizing their promise. The articles focus on three populations of students: twice-exceptional students—gifted students who are at risk for poor development due to difficulties in learning and attention;

gifted students who face gender issues that inhibit their ability to achieve or develop socially and emotionally, and students who are economically disadvantaged and at risk for dropping out of school. Baum summarizes research indicating that each of these groups of youngsters is affected by one or more barriers to development, and the most poignant of these barriers are identification strategies, lack of awareness of consequences of co-morbidity, deficit thinking in program design, and lack of appropriate social and emotional support. She ends her introduction with a series of thoughtful questions focusing on future directions in this critical area.

Sidney Moon introduces the seminal articles on the social and emotional development of and counseling for gifted children by acknowledging the contributions of the National Association for Gifted Children's task forces that have examined social/emotional issues. The first task force, formed in 2000 and called the Social and Emotional Issues Task Force, completed its work in 2002 by publishing an edited book, *The Social and Emotional Development of Gifted Children: What Do We Know?* This volume provides an extensive review of the literature on the social and emotional development of gifted children (Neihart, Reis, Robinson, & Moon, 2002). Moon believes that the seminal studies in the area of the social and emotional development and counseling illustrate both the strengths and the weaknesses of the current literature on social and emotional issues in the field of gifted education. These articles bring increased attention to the affective needs of special populations of gifted students, such as underachievers, who are at risk for failure to achieve their potential, but also point to the need for more empirical studies on "what works" with these students, both in terms of preventative strategies and more intensive interventions. She acknowledges that although good counseling models have been developed, they need to be rigorously evaluated to determine their effectiveness under disparate conditions, and calls for additional research on the affective and counseling interventions with specific subtypes of gifted students such as Asian Americans, African Americans, and twice-exceptional students. Moon also strongly encourages researchers in the field of gifted education to collaborate with researchers from affective fields such as personal and social psychology, counseling psychology, family therapy, and psychiatry to learn to intervene most effectively with gifted individuals with problems and to learn better how to help all gifted persons achieve optimal social, emotional, and personal development.

ARTISTICALLY AND CREATIVELY TALENTED STUDENTS (VOLUMES 9, 10)

Enid Zimmerman introduces the volume on talent development in the visual and performing arts with a summary of articles about students who are talented in music, dance, visual arts, and spatial, kinesthetic, and expressive areas. Major themes that appear in the articles include perceptions by parents, students, and teachers that often focus on concerns related to nature versus nurture in arts talent development; research about the crystallizing experiences of artistically talented students; collaboration between school and community members about identification of talented art students from diverse backgrounds; and leadership issues related to empowering teachers of talented arts students. They all are concerned to some extent with teacher, parent, and student views about educating artistically talented students. Included also are discussions about identification of talented students from urban, suburban, and rural environments. Zimmerman believes that in this particular area, a critical need exists for research about the impact of educational opportunities, educational settings, and the role of art teachers on the development of artistically talented students. The impact of the standards and testing movement and its relationship to the education of talented students in the visual and performing arts is an area greatly in need of investigation. Research also is needed about students' backgrounds, personalities, gender orientations, skill development, and cognitive and affective abilities as well as cross-cultural contexts and the impact of global and popular culture on the education of artistically talented students. The compelling case study with which she introduces this volume sets the stage for the need for this research.

Donald Treffinger introduces reflections on articles about creativity by discussing the following five core themes that express the collective efforts of researchers to grasp common conceptual and theoretical challenges associated with creativity. The themes include **Definitions** (how we define giftedness, talent, or creativity), **Characteristics** (the indicators of giftedness and creativity in people), **Justification** (Why is creativity important in education?), **Assessment** of creativity, and the ways we **Nurture** creativity. Treffinger also discusses the expansion of knowledge, the changes that have occurred, the search for answers, and the questions that still remain. In the early years of interest of creativity research, Treffinger believed that considerable discussion existed about whether it was possible to foster creativity through training or instruction. He reports that over the last 50 years, educators have learned that deliberate efforts to nurture creativity are possible (e.g., Torrance, 1987), and further extends this line of inquiry by asking the key question, "What works best, for whom, and under what conditions?" Treffinger summarizes the challenges faced by educators who try to nurture the development of creativity through effective teaching and to ask which experiences will have the greatest impact, as these will help to determine our ongoing lines of research, development, and training initiatives.

EVALUATION AND PUBLIC POLICY (VOLUMES 11, 12)

Carolyn Callahan introduces the seminal articles on evaluation and suggests that this important component neglected by experts in the field of gifted education for at least the last three decades can be a plea for important work by both evaluators and practitioners. She divides the seminal literature on evaluation, and in particular the literature on the evaluation of gifted programs into four categories, those which (a) provide theory and/or practical guidelines, (b) describe or report on specific program evaluations, (c) provide stimuli for the discussion of issues surrounding the evaluation process, and (d) suggest new research on the evaluation process. Callahan concludes with a challenge indicating work to be done and the opportunity for experts to make valuable contributions to increased effectiveness and efficiency of programs for the gifted.

James Gallagher provides a call-to-arms in the seminal articles he introduces on public policy by raising some of the most challenging questions in the field. Gallagher suggests that as a field, we need to come to some consensus about stronger interventions and consider how we react to accusations of elitism. He believes that our field could be doing a great deal more with additional targeted resources supporting the general education teacher and the development of specialists in gifted education, and summarizes that our failure to fight in the public arena for scarce resources may raise again the question posed two decades ago by Renzulli (1980), looking toward 1990: "Will the gifted child movement be alive and well in 2010?"

CONCLUSION

What can we learn from an examination of our field and the seminal articles that have emerged over the last few decades? First, we must **respect the past** by acknowledging the times in which articles were written and the shoulders of those persons upon whom we stand as we continue to create and develop our field. An old proverb tells us that when we drink from the well, we must remember to acknowledge those who dug the well, and in our field the early articles represent the seeds that grew our field. Next, we must **celebrate the present** and the exciting work and new directions in our field and the knowledge that is now accepted as a common core. Last, we must **embrace the future** by understanding that there is no finished product when it comes to research on gifted and talented children and how we are best able to meet their unique needs. Opportunities abound in the work reported in this series, but many questions remain. A few things seem clear. Action in the future should be based on both qualitative and quantitative research as well as longitudinal studies, and what we have completed only scratches the surface regarding the many variables and issues that still need to be explored. Research is needed that suggests positive changes that will lead to more inclusive programs that recognize the talents and gifts of diverse students in our country. When this occurs, future teachers and researchers in gifted education will find answers that can be embraced by educators, communities, and families, and the needs of all talented and gifted students will be more effectively met in their classrooms by teachers who have been trained to develop their students' gifts and talents.

We also need to consider carefully how we work with the field of education in general. As technology emerges and improves, new opportunities will become available to us. Soon, all students should be able to have their curricular needs preassessed before they begin any new curriculum unit. Soon, the issue of keeping students on grade-level material when they are many grades ahead should disappear as technology enables us to pinpoint students' strengths. Will chronological grades be eliminated? The choices we have when technology enables us to learn better what students already know presents exciting scenarios for the future, and it is imperative that we advocate carefully for multiple opportunities for these students, based on their strengths and interests, as well as a challenging core curriculum. Parents, educators, and professionals who care about these special populations need to become politically active to draw attention to the unique needs of these students, and researchers need to conduct the experimental studies that can prove the efficacy of providing talent development options as well as opportunities for healthy social and emotional growth.

For any field to continue to be vibrant and to grow, new voices must be heard, and new players sought. A great opportunity is available in our field; for as we continue to advocate for gifted and talented students, we can also play important roles in the changing educational reform movement. We can continue to work to achieve more challenging opportunities for all students while we fight to maintain gifted, talented, and enrichment programs. We can continue our advocacy for differentiation through acceleration, individual curriculum opportunities, and a continuum of advanced curriculum and personal support opportunities. The questions answered and those raised in this volume of seminal articles can help us to move forward as a field. We hope those who read the series will join us in this exciting journey.

REFERENCES

Baldwin, A.Y. (1977). Tests do underpredict: A case study. *Phi Delta Kappan, 58,* 620-621.

Gallagher, J. J. (1979). Issues in education for the gifted. In A. H. Passow (Ed.), *The gifted and the talented: Their education and development* (pp. 28-44). Chicago: University of Chicago Press.

Guilford, J. E. (1967). *The nature of human intelligence.* New York: McGraw-Hill.

Marland, S. P., Jr. (1972). *Education of the gifted and talented: Vol. 1. Report to the Congress of the United States by the U.S. Commissioner of Education.* Washington, DC: U.S. Government Printing Office.

Neihart, M., Reis, S., Robinson, N., & Moon, S. M. (Eds.). (2002). *The social and emotional development of gifted children: What do we know?* Waco, TX: Prufrock.

Renzulli, J. S. (1978). What makes giftedness? Reexamining a definition. *Phi Delta Kappan, 60*(5), 180-184.

Renzulli, J. S. (1980). Will the gifted child movement be alive and well in 1990? *Gifted Child Quarterly, 24*(1), 3-9. **[See Vol. 12.]**

Renzulli, J. (1982). Dear Mr. and Mrs. Copernicus: We regret to inform you . . . *Gifted Child Quarterly, 26*(1), 11-14. **[See Vol. 2.]**

Renzulli, J. S. (Ed.). (1986). *Systems and models for developing programs for the gifted and talented.* Mansfield Center, CT: Creative Learning Press.

Renzulli, J. S., & Delcourt, M. A. B. (1986). The legacy and logic of research on the identification of gifted persons. *Gifted Child Quarterly, 30*(1), 20-23. **[See Vol. 2.]**

Renzulli J., & Hartman, R. (1971). Scale for rating behavioral characteristics of superior students. *Exceptional Children, 38,* 243-248.

Ross, P. (1993). *National excellence: A case for developing America's talent.* Washington, DC: U.S. Department of Education, Government Printing Office.

Sternberg, R. J. (1982). Nonentrenchment in the assessment of intellectual giftedness. *Gifted Child Quarterly, 26*(2), 63-67. **[See Vol. 2.]**

Tannenbaum, A. J. (1983). *Gifted children: Psychological and educational perspectives.* New York: Macmillan.

Torrance, E. P. (1984). The role of creativity in identification of the gifted and talented. *Gifted Child Quarterly, 28*(4), 153-156. **[See Vols. 2 and 10.]**

Torrance, E. P. (1987). Recent trends in teaching children and adults to think creatively. In S. G. Isaksen (Ed.), *Frontiers of creativity research: Beyond the basics* (pp. 204-215). Buffalo, NY: Bearly Limited.

Introduction to Identification of Students for Gifted and Talented Programs

Joseph S. Renzulli

The University of Connecticut

It is better to have imprecise answers to the right questions than precise answers to the wrong questions.

—Donald Campbell

How to identify students for participation in programs for the gifted and talented continues to be one of the most widely discussed and debated topics in the field. The fourteen seminal articles from *Gifted Child Quarterly* in this volume represent a cross-section of research and commentary about key ideas and concepts that attempt to lend both wisdom and clarity to important concerns about identification, and of course, these ideas also relate to the conceptions of giftedness discussed in volume one of the series. Both theoretical and practical relationships exist between the definitions and conceptions of giftedness and talent and issues related to identification. This relationship represents a good point of departure for two of the main issues that should guide all identification processes and which are discussed in varying contexts by the authors of articles about identification.

THEORY-BASED IDENTIFICATION

The first point is that how one defines or conceptualizes giftedness should be the theoretical rationale underlying an identification system, and this rationale, in turn, should guide the selection criteria for identification instruments and the ways in which instruments are used in identification practices. Conceptions of giftedness can be viewed as existing along a continuum ranging from a very conservative or restricted view of giftedness to a more flexible or multi-dimensional approach. The conservative view, which dominated thought and therefore identification practices throughout the early part of the past century, focused almost exclusively on IQ test scores or other measures of cognitive ability. It was not uncommon to observe IQ cut-off scores as being the sole criterion for entrance into gifted programs, and many of the guidelines and regulations developed by state agencies and school districts reflected this conservative tradition. Even in cases where multi-criteria were used as the first step (screening) in a two-phase identification process, the second step (selection) continued to be based on individual intelligence test scores. This approach has frequently fallen prey to what I have sometimes referred to as a "multi-criteria smoke screen" because it gives the impression of examining a broader range of indicators of potential, but in most cases high grades in regular schoolwork, teacher ratings, or other criteria only served the purpose of earning the student a "ticket" to take an individual intelligence test. This approach is mendacious because it gives the *appearance* of multi-criteria identification, when in reality it is one-dimensional, and therefore very restrictive when it comes to the potential value of a broader range of criteria. And the "gems of wisdom" that might be uncovered in the process of collecting a broader range of identification information are, in effect, thrown into the trash if the student does not reach a predetermined cut-off level on a cognitive ability test.

Jack Birch points out this dilemma in his article titled "Is *Any* Identification Procedure Necessary?" He suggests that " . . . we need to explore the broader context within which the child functions and which includes social, personal, and cultural factors which contribute much to the shaping of academic abilities, limitations, special interests and potentials" (Birch, 1984, p. 158). Other authors of these seminal articles echo this message (e.g., Callahan, 1982; Torrance, 1984; Borland & Wright, 1994), and a general theme of the section calls into question over-reliance on intelligence test scores. Persons contributing to this section are not arguing that intelligence test scores are *un*important! Most agree that intelligence tests and other cognitive ability tests provide us with one very important form of information about one dimension of a young person's potential, mainly in the areas of verbal and analytic skills. Nor are these authors arguing that cognitive ability tests should be dropped from the identification process. Rather, the argument is that (1) other indicators of potential should be used for identification, (2) these indicators should be given equal consideration when it comes to making final decisions about which students will be candidates for special services, and (3) in the final analysis, it is the thoughtful judgment of knowledgeable professionals rather than instruments and cut-off scores that should guide selection decisions.

Another issue addressed by these authors is what has been variously referred to as the distinction between (1) convergent and divergent thinking (Guilford, 1967; Torrance, 1984), (2) entrenchment and non-entrenchment (Sternberg, 1982a, 1982b), and (3) schoolhouse giftedness vs. creative/productive giftedness (Renzulli, 1982; Renzulli & Delcourt, 1986). Conservatives have generally favored explaining giftedness in terms of performance that is more convergent or entrenched and of the schoolhouse variety.

Schoolhouse giftedness is the kind most easily measured by standardized ability tests and performance in traditional curricular pursuits, and therefore the type most conveniently used for selecting students for special programs. The competencies young people display on cognitive ability tests are exactly the kinds of abilities most valued in traditional school learning situations, especially those situations that focus on analytic skills rather than creative or practical skills. Research has shown a high correlation between schoolhouse giftedness and the likelihood of getting high grades in school. Research has also shown that superior lesson learning and test taking remain stable over time. These results should lead us to some very obvious conclusions about schoolhouse giftedness: it exists in varying degrees; it easily can be identified through standardized tests, teacher ratings, course grades, and informal assessment techniques; and we should therefore do everything in our power to make appropriate modifications for students who have the ability to cover regular curricular material at advanced rates and levels of understanding than their age peers. We should also remember, however, that the abilities people display in traditional lesson-learning situations bear a striking resemblance to the factors measured on typical cognitive ability tests; in today's atmosphere of high-stakes testing and the corresponding emphasis that is given to "test prep," this relationship grows stronger. Both research and our everyday experiences (i.e., common sense) verify the strong relationships between efficient lesson learning and high test scores. An examination of rapid progress through the regular curriculum (as determined by course grades and teacher judgment) should be a major consideration in identification and service delivery decisions regardless of standardized test scores.

Although schoolhouse giftedness should be valued and accommodated in any service delivery model, mainly through curriculum modification and replacement techniques, at lease equal attention should be devoted to creative productive giftedness. Creative productive giftedness describes those aspects of human activity and involvement where a premium is placed on the development of original ideas, where student interests are taken into consideration, where investigative methodology is a central focus of learning, and where products, artistic expressions, and areas of knowledge that are purposefully designed to have an impact on one or more target audiences is the rationale for organizing learning experiences. Learning situations that are designed to promote creative productive giftedness emphasize the use and *application* of knowledge and thinking processes in an integrated, inductive, and real-problem oriented manner. The role of the student is transformed from that of a learner of prescribed lessons and consumer of information to one in which he or she approximates the *modus operandi* of the first-hand inquirer. These types of student involvement are consistent with the roles that gifted persons have played in society.

The importance of creative productive giftedness raises critical questions so far as identification is concerned. Whereas lesson learning giftedness, which is mainly accounted for in measures of cognitive ability, tends to remain stable over time, persons do not always display maximum creativity, task commitment, or other traits that lead to creative productive giftedness. Highly creative and productive people have peaks and valleys of high-level output. Some persons have commented that the valleys are as necessary as the peaks, because they allow for reflection, regeneration, and the accumulation of input for subsequent endeavors. Similarly, creative productive giftedness tends to be contextual or domain specific. While there certainly have been a small number of "Renaissance" men and women who have gained recognition for work in several fields, the overwhelming number of persons who have been recognized for their outstanding contributions have almost always achieved in a single field or domain. The history of human accomplishment, and especially research about the accomplishments of persons who have made important contributions to the arts, sciences, and all other areas of human progress (Renzulli, 1978, 1986) tells us that divergent thinking, non-entrenchment, and creative productive giftedness are types of giftedness that are most valued by society. Once again, these types of giftedness are not as easily identified as schoolhouse giftedness, but the authors of this section seem to agree that the convenience of easy and so-called objective measurements should not be the driving force behind an identification system. In a certain sense, making a decision to determine giftedness on the basis of a single, one hour cognitive ability test is about as subjective as one can get!

Implications about the temporal and contextual nature of creative productive giftedness are clear, but perhaps discomforting, at least to persons who have a need to state unequivocally on the first day of school that a student is gifted or not gifted. Although conceptions of giftedness have changed dramatically over the past quarter century, conservative ideologies still have appeal to persons who believe that giftedness is an absolute construct (you are either gifted or not gifted, and nothing will ever change your status). In some cases, conservatives give the guru-like illusion that they have within themselves a magical power to proclaim whether or not a child is gifted. If you ask a conservative what is the basis for his or her determination that a person "is truly gifted" in the absolute sense, his/her response almost always falls into one or a combination of two categories. The first response usually alludes to IQ scores. This response is frequently followed by a description of something the youngster did—wrote an outstanding story, developed an Internet web site, demonstrated leadership in a particular situation. These accomplishments of young people draw upon something they did or produced, and in recognizing productivity as a manifestation of giftedness it is self-evident that characteristics in addition to cognitive ability come into play. In some cases non-cognitive characteristics such as motivation, creativity, passionate interests, physical and mental energy, and a sense of power to change things are more influential in carrying out complicated projects than cognitive abilities. No one, to my knowledge, has ever said, "you have to produce a product to be gifted," and as mentioned above, even conservatives allude to productivity in making a case for who is and is not gifted. But products created by young people serve as vehicles through which gifted behaviors are developed and enhanced, and thus their role is an important part of the rationale of the developmentalists for a broader set of identification criteria.

Developmentalists, persons at the opposite end of the continuum from conservatives, might best be described as those who believe that giftedness is not "fixed" in an individual, but rather is developed in certain people (not all people), at certain times (not all the time), and under certain circumstances (not in all circumstances). And contrary to accusations of the conservatives, developmentalists do not argue that "all children are gifted" or that we can create giftedness in all young people. They do, however, argue and support through research (Reis & Renzulli, 1982) that we can develop gifted behaviors in a larger proportion of the school population than the three to five percent usually selected by test scores.

What are the implications for identification between the conservative and developmental points of view? Conservatives clearly have the appearance of objectivity on their side; they also have appeal to regulation writers and those who like the administrative "tidiness" that makes test score cut-off approaches appealing. And those seductive story tellers who pander to parents on the speaker's circuit would lose a good part of their consulting fees if they couldn't assure audiences that they know with certainty who is "truly gifted."

The authors in this section are in universal agreement about broader conceptions of giftedness and a developmental perspective that provides more flexible identification procedures. But they also realize that "body count" funding formulas (x dollars per identified gifted child) and concerns about objectivity require creative approaches to identification. In recent years the research on broadened conceptions of giftedness has led several state departments of education to introduce more flexibility into their guidelines, and even in states with relatively rigid guidelines, there are greater efforts to provide waivers and interpret guidelines more flexibly.

RELATIONSHIP BETWEEN
PROGRAM AND IDENTIFICATION

Feldhusen, Asher, and Hoover (1984) point out what might be called the golden rule of identification—"The careful determination of program goals will set the direction for the entire identification process" (1984, p. 149). At the secondary level most programs are organized around specific domains or aptitudes, and this focus on content area goals has identification implications. Benbow and Minor's research shows that " . . . global indicators of intellectual functioning may exclude too many nonverbally gifted students, who appear to be less balanced than verbally gifted students in their cognitive development" (1990, p. 21). If a program is based, for example, on performance in accelerated mathematics courses, then it makes sense to use mathematics aptitude test scores and math grades as a central focus in the identification process. The same can be said for other special aptitudes (e.g., arts, creative writing, technology). But if creative productivity is part of intended goals and outcomes within specific content areas, then a blend of grades and aptitude scores can be combined with samples of student work, teacher ratings, and other criteria that reflect how students have applied their aptitudes to situations in which creative productivity was an intended outcome. It is difficult to imagine, for example, how an art program would not use portfolios or a drama program would not use auditions (as opposed to test scores) to determine the best possible candidates. In certain areas, performance criteria may be the single best form of identification information. Although teacher ratings have emerged as a widely used identification criterion, Clark's study of visually talented students raises questions about teacher ratings in this specific performance area: "One of the interesting findings of this research is a lack of correlation between age and performance on drawing tasks and teacher ratings" (1989, p. 102).

At the elementary level most programs do not have a specific aptitude focus; the typical pull-out program is usually a combination of various thinking skill activities and teacher-selected units that deal with topics not ordinarily covered in the regular curriculum. Regardless of what takes place in the program, the larger goals and outcomes of the program should influence identification decisions. Does the program merely strive to increase students' knowledge acquisition? Is creative productivity and the application of knowledge a major outcome? Are leadership skills and affective development important goals? Will a blend of students with various strengths enhance the interactions that take place in the program? If, as Rimm (1984) points out, a broad range of interests, independence, and imagination are important indicators of giftedness, then it is equally important to take these traits into consideration in the identification process.

AT-RISK POPULATIONS

A theme running throughout several of the articles in this section is that traditional identification procedures " . . . have failed to respond to our society's diversity by adequately identifying and serving gifted students who are economically disadvantaged, especially students from racial and ethnic minority groups" (Borland & Wright, 1994). Almost all authors have offered suggestions for broader identification criteria, and whether or not they have directly addressed diverse groups, their recommendations certainly relate to this very crucial issue facing our field. McKenzie (1986) called attention to the racial and socioeconomic bias in standardized achievement and intelligence tests and warns that such tests may actually reinforce existing inequalities in the selection of children from diverse populations. His survey of several hundred school districts shows the relationship between gifted program participation and race, per pupil spending, socioeconomic status, and property value. Although we have long known about these factors influencing the inclusion of diverse populations in gifted programs, most writers on the subject are in agreement that there is need for more research that deals directly with the effectiveness of alternative identification procedures.

One study that deals directly with this challenge was conducted by Borland and Wright (1994). Using a population of severely disadvantaged inner city first and second grade students, the authors designed a multi-phase study that examined standardized assessment, non-traditional assessment, and teacher nomination. Parent input, classroom observation, and performance tasks were also used. Although the authors point out that the process they developed is time- and labor-intensive, they nevertheless have shown that a valid and research supported identification process based on site-appropriate methods such as observation, dynamic assessment, and examples of best performance can successfully identify economically disadvantaged participants for gifted programs.

OTHER ISSUES AND CONCERNS

A number of articles in this section deal with additional issues related to identification. Colangelo and Brower (1987) investigated the effects of labeling in family dynamics. They found a difference between immediate and long-term family effects of having a child labeled as "gifted"; while siblings came to terms with the designation of a family member, the identified students expressed uneasiness about the effects of the label on other members of the family. These authors point out the need for additional research on family factors associated with labeling. Callahan (1982) also addresses the labeling issue when she comments on how "winners" and "losers" are sometimes viewed as the outcome of formal identification processes; however, her concern is extended to perceptions within the peer group rather than the family. She also discusses important concerns about how teachers sometimes are affected by formal labeling and designated services. Classroom teachers may fail to make necessary accommodations in the regular curriculum because they assume that " . . . the 'giftedness' of the child is 'taken care of' in the resource room . . ." (p. 17). Birch (1984) also comments on the labeling issue (which he calls "typing") in yet another context. He argues that such "typing . . . can be a powerful deterrent and strong barrier to the recognition of individual characteristics of each child, the features and attributes that should guide educational interpretations and adaptations"

(p. 158). If we are to avoid one-size-fits-all gifted programs, Birch's suggestion for psychoeducational assessment that examines interests, learning styles, and other potentialities should be part of the equation that leads to more individualized programming directed at talent development.

CONCLUSIONS, CHALLENGES, AND FUTURE DIRECTIONS

The articles on identification are restricted to publications in *Gifted Child Quarterly* over a period of twelve years, beginning in 1982 and extending through 1994. A great deal has obviously been written prior to and subsequent to this window through which we have been looking, and there are other important articles, books, and research reports that have appeared in other journals. Interested persons can gain a broader historical perspective on identification by examining the many citations in the present collection of articles, and conducting electronic literature searches that will reveal literally hundreds of books, articles, technical reports, and state and district guidelines for identification. The authors of this collection of *GCQ* articles have dealt with the majority of critical issues that surround the always controversial and frequently contentious age-old question of who is gifted and who is not! A few general conclusions emerge with a fair degree of consistency among this group of writers.

First, all agree that a single intelligence or other cognitive ability score is not the best way to identify gifted students. This is not to say that such information is unimportant in making selection decisions. Rather, a combination of background information should be used; this information should include both test and non-test criteria, and all criteria should be given comparable "weight" in the identification process (see comments above about the multiple-criteria smoke screen). It is important to remember that all criteria used in an identification process are only information, and it is people rather than information that make decisions. An identification process, therefore, should give as much attention to the ways in which information will be used, the relationship between identification and program services, and the training provided to persons taking part in the identification process. In our effort to be "objective" we have often succumbed to turning decision making over to instruments rather than recognizing the importance of human judgment in making selection decisions. And when it comes to information and its use, it is important to remember that there are two categories of information that need to be considered.

The first type, *status information*, consists of test scores, previous grades or accomplishments, teacher ratings, and anything else we can "put down on paper" beforehand that tells us something about a person's traits and potentials. Status information is undoubtedly the best way for identifying students with high levels of schoolhouse giftedness, and it can also be used to identify a talent pool of students who achieve at above-average levels in traditionally measured school achievement. But the temporal and contextual nature of high levels of creative productivity requires that we look for these behaviors *within* situations where such behaviors are displayed and hopefully encouraged. Thus, a second type of information must have a place in the identification process. I call this type *action information*, and it can best be defined as the type of dynamic interactions that take place when a person becomes extremely interested in or excited about a particular topic, area of study, issue, idea, or event that takes place within the school or the non-school environment. In a certain sense, what I described as action information is not unlike the currently popular concepts called dynamic assessment or performance-based assessment, although action information is for proactive decision making rather than evaluation of student progress. These interactions occur when students come into contact with or are influenced by persons, concepts, or particular pieces of knowledge. The influence of the interaction may be relatively limited, or it may have a highly positive and extremely motivating effect on certain individuals. If the influence is strong enough and positive enough to promote further exploration and follow-up at high levels of creative or investigative activity on the part of an individual or group of students with a common interest, then we may say that a dynamic interaction has taken place. The level to which high level follow-up is pursued is dependent on youngsters' abilities, motivation, and creativity; at this juncture the teacher's role as a talent developer is crucial. It is this role, in fact, that should be a major part of teacher training in our field.

By definition, action information cannot be pre-documented; and therefore, a comprehensive and responsive identification process must have vehicles for systematically obtaining and using the dynamic interactions that may warrant one or more follow-up services. Teacher awareness of this component of an identification system and training in how to spot dynamic interactions that may lead to follow-up or referral opportunities is important for effectively using an action information component in the identification process. Equally important is the flexibility necessary for allowing students thus identified to revolve into services that will capitalize on the "turn on" that brought them to our attention. To translate the action information concept into practice, my colleagues Sally Reis and Linda Smith and I developed the Revolving Door Identification Model (RDIM, Renzulli, Reis, & Smith, 1981). The essence of this model is to provide a "talent pool" of above average–ability students with a broad variety of general enrichment experiences, and use the ways in which students *respond* to these experiences to determine who and in which areas of study students should "revolve" into more advanced enrichment opportunities. In addition to the general enrichment provided in special program situations, we also trained classroom teachers to use a form called the Action Information Message so that they could serve as referral agents whenever students reacted in highly positive ways to regular classroom experiences. Although this approach to identification departs significantly from traditional practices, it is consistent with the suggestions of many authors of these seminal articles, and its effectiveness has been documented by a series of research studies and field tests in schools with widely varying socioeconomic levels and program organizational patterns (Reis & Renzulli, 1982).

A second conclusion, and one that will no doubt be the object of much controversy for as long as our field exists is how we use the word "gifted." Is the word best used as a noun or an adjective? Is a person gifted in the absolute sense (what I have sometimes referred as the "golden chromosome theory"), or do we develop gifted behaviors in certain people, at certain times, under certain circumstances? Is it more appropriate to say that a fifth-grade boy or girl is "gifted," or are we better off saying that she or he is a gifted young writer or scientist or violinist? These questions have important implications for the important relationship that should exist between identification practices and the ways in which we serve targeted students. If students must be predetermined to be gifted *before* any special services are made available (the absolutist approach), we certainly have the administrative tidiness that is often required by state guidelines, especially in states that reimburse school districts on the basis of the number of formally identified gifted students. But if we are looking for students whose potentials might not show up through traditional tests or other forms of status information, or students whose high potentials may not be triggered until they are exposed to challenging opportunities, then we may be trading off administrative tidiness for a flexible identification system that embraces action information. A more flexible system also takes into account the crucial roles played by interests, creativity, task commitment, and affective traits that are best discovered contextually and through the types of dynamic interactions discussed above.

This second conclusion has policy implications for resource allocation and is, once again, related to policies in states that reimburse schools districts based on the number of pre-identified students, what I sometimes refer to as "the body count states." It also is related to the underrepresentation of minorities in special programs for the gifted, mainly because these students do not achieve at as high levels as majority students on traditional measures of cognitive aptitude. Typically, the more affluent school districts receive larger amounts of reimbursement because of higher test scores. Recommended variations in funding formulas in the body count states are often viewed with suspicion because of a fear of runaway costs, and even advocates of more flexible identification practices are cautious because they fear "losing" what has already gained in legislative allocations.

There is a way out of the funding formula dilemma without endangering a loss of present financial commitments, and this approach will also help to bring some degree of equity to districts that serve high proportions of at-risk students. By allocating funds based on total district enrollment each district will be eligible for a fixed amount of funding each year. The success of this approach, however, is not without its potential pitfalls! All districts applying for reimbursement must prepare proposals that show an identification system that clearly focuses on finding students who are most in need of special program opportunities and services, and a carefully articulated designation of services must be specified. Although funding levels are determined on the basis of total district enrollment, it is important that the monies be budgeted in a separate account (rather than the general school budget), that the majority of funds be used for program-designated personnel, and that a comprehensive evaluation design be built into the guidelines for program proposals. Without these budgetary safeguards and targeted personnel requirements, funds might end up in an enrichment "slush fund" that pays for field trips, uniforms for the band, or other dubious uses of supplementary funds.

A great deal of progress has been made in the identification of gifted students over the past quarter century. These articles have addressed both the challenges faced and possible solutions to some of these challenges. New approaches that address the equity issue, policies and practices that respect new theories about human potential and conceptions of giftedness, and a continuous commitment to research-based identification practices are still needed. And although scientifically defensible identification practices should be a major focus of future investigations, it is important to keep in mind that some of the characteristics that have led to the recognition of history's most gifted contributors are not always as measurable as others. We need to continue our search for those elusive things that are left over after everything explainable has been explained, to realize that giftedness is culturally and contextually imbedded in all human activity, and most of all, we need to value the value of even those things that we cannot yet explain.

REFERENCES

Benbow, C. P., & Minor, L. L. (1990). Cognitive profiles of verbally and mathematically precocious students: Implications for identification of the gifted. *Gifted Child Quarterly, 34*(1), 21-26. **[See Vol. 2, p. 87.]**

Birch, J. W. (1984). Is any identification procedure necessary? *Gifted Child Quarterly, 28*(4), 157-161. **[See Vol. 2, p. 1.]**

Borland, J. H., & Wright, L. (1994). Identifying young, potentially gifted, economically disadvantaged students. *Gifted Child Quarterly, 38*(4), 164-171. **[See Vol. 2, p. 25.]**

Callahan, C. M. (1982). Myth: There must be "winners" and "losers" in identification and programming! *Gifted Child Quarterly, 26*(1), 17-19. **[See Vol. 2, p. 11.]**

Clark, G. (1989). Screening and identifying students talented in the visual arts: Clark's Drawing Abilities Test. *Gifted Child Quarterly, 33*(3), 98-105. **[See Vol. 2, p. 101.]**

Colangelo, N., & Brower, P. (1987). Labeling gifted youngsters: Long-term impact on families. *Gifted Child Quarterly, 31*(2), 75-78. **[See Vol. 2, p. 137.]**

Feldhusen, J. F., Asher, J. W., & Hoover, S. M. (1984). Problems in the identification of giftedness, talent, or ability. *Gifted Child Quarterly, 28*(4), 149-151. **[See Vol. 2, p. 79.]**

McKenzie, J. A. (1986). The influence of identification practices, race and SES on the identification of gifted students. *Gifted Child Quarterly, 30*(2), 93-95. **[See Vol. 2, p. 131.]**

Reis, S. M., & Renzulli, J. S. (1982). A research report on the revolving door identification model: A case for the broadened conception of giftedness. *Phi Delta Kappan, 63*(9), 619-620.

Renzulli, J. S. (1978). What makes giftedness? Reexamining a definition. *Phi Delta Kappan, 60*(5), 180-184.

Renzulli, J. S. (1982). Myth: The gifted constitute 3–5% of the population (Dear Mr. and Mrs. Copernicus: We regret to inform you. . .) *Gifted Child Quarterly, 26*(1), 11-14. **[See Vol. 2, p. 63.]**

Renzulli, J. S. (1986). The three-rings conception of giftedness: A developmental model for creative productivity. In R. J. Sternberg & J. E. Davidson (Eds.), *Conceptions of giftedness* (pp. 53-92). New York: Cambridge University Press.

Renzulli, J. S., & Delcourt, M. A. B. (1986). The legacy and logic of research on the identification of gifted persons. *Gifted Child Quarterly, 30*(1), 20-23. **[See Vol. 2, p. 71.]**

Renzulli, J. S., Reis, S. M., & Smith, L. H. (1981). *Revolving door identification model guidebook.* Mansfield Center, CT: Creative Learning Press.

Rimm, S. (1984). The characteristics approach: Identification and beyond. *Gifted Child Quarterly, 28*(4), 181-187. **[See Vol. 2, p. 117.]**

Sternberg, R. J. (1982a). Nonentrenchment in the assessment of intellectual giftedness. *Gifted Child Quarterly, 26*(2), 63-67. **[See Vol. 2, p. 43.]**

Sternberg, R. J. (1982b). Lies we live by: Misapplication of tests in identifying the gifted. *Gifted Child Quarterly, 26*(4), 157-161. **[See Vol. 2, p. 53.]**

Torrance, E. P. (1984). The role of creativity in identification of the gifted and talented. *Gifted Child Quarterly, 28*(4), 153-156. **[See Vol. 2, p. 17.]**

1

Is Any Identification Procedure Necessary?

Jack W. Birch

It certainly is advisable to locate gifted children and to see that they receive individually appropriate education. However, that does not mean that it is necessary or even desirable to institutionalize a process called "identification," especially one that embodies weaknesses and dangerously destructive tendencies. The prevailing "identification → placement" paradigm needs to be replaced by the preferred "assess ↔ educate" model, one in which the separate "identification" step is replaced by curriculum-imbedded and curriculum-determinitive processes for surfacing and serving gifted students.

The "identification" commonly practiced has negative and limiting implications for the education of gifted children and youth. The most widely used "identification" method is narrowly conceived. Often, in reality, it belies or markedly warps its published purposes, results in the misuse of psychological tests, leaves out potentially useful contributions from professionals and other concerned adults, and has little or no direct linkage with instruction or, more broadly, with individualized education. It is difficult to justify the use of an "identification" process that is loaded with such weaknesses. It is even

Editor's Note: From Birch, J. W. (1984). Is *any* identification procedure necessary? *Gifted Child Quarterly, 28*(4), 157-161. © 1984 National Association for Gifted Children. Reprinted with permission.

more difficult to justify it when the very underlying rationale for a separate, gatekeeper-type "identification" could be displaced with profit by processes inherent in the "assess ↔ educate" model, in which locating and educating the children are designed to more than interface, but to interact.

First, the negative and limiting implications of the prevailing "identification" scheme will be pointed out. That will set the stage for an introduction to the location of gifted children as accomplished by the "assess ↔ educate" approach. Finally, five very important principles for school districts regarding identification policies and practices will be presented, their rationales being drawn from the previous material.

IDENTIFICATION AS VERIFICATION

Most of what is called "identification" of gifted children in the United States today is really the verification that a child is able to earn above a certain score in the upper range on an intelligence test. Relatively few school systems really proceed in an orderly way to try to find (that is, "identify") all of their gifted children. Instead, reliance is placed on "screening" by group intelligence tests and on referral by interested but untrained parents and teachers, using informal appraisal and school achievement (tests and grades) to suggest individual children for consideration for special programs. The administration of an individual psychological test like the Wechsler or the Binet then *verifies* or *does not verify* the judgment of the persons who nominated the child in the first place. Thus, the very use of the term *identification* is at best misleading and at worst downright incorrect (Sellin & Birch, 1980).

THE "MULTIPLE CRITERIA" CHIMERA

It is common to see and hear claims that "multiple criteria" procedures are used (even required!) to "identify" gifted pupils. To validate such assertions, regulations are printed. They state that parent and teacher nominations, plus grades in school and achievement test scores, are to be considered along with socio-economic and cultural differences, interests and talents, and scores on intelligence tests. In reality, however, too many times there is really only one criterion, namely, a break-point score on an individually administered intelligence test. That is commonly an intelligence quotient of 130, with a possibility of allowing a range down to 125. "Identification" has degenerated, for all its claims about embracing many factors, to no more than a single score on one intelligence test. Despite the array of other data that might be accumulated about a child, the *"is gifted"* or *"is not gifted"* decision comes down to falling on one side or the other of the intelligence quotient break-point (Kirschenbaum, 1983).

It is serious enough that decisions of life-long import are made about children by reference to one score on one test done by a psychologist who often knows little else other than that the youngster is a candidate for "identification." Unfortunately, this kind of action has other worrisome consequences, too.

THE "CUT-OFF LINE" FALLACY AND DISTORTION

Paradoxically, almost everyone who uses the prevailing means of "identification" also knows that they are perpetuating a fallacy and encouraging a distortion. The fallacy is that there is a definite natural intelligence quotient point dividing gifted children from others. That simply is not true. Rather, the point of demarkation always represents a decision of convenience, not one that "carves nature at its joints" (Reynolds, 1978).

As to the distortion, it is one of social policy. The point was made very plainly by Newland (1976) when he spelled out how a rational cut-off, based on societal need, could be determined if a locality, a state or a nation would first determine just how many gifted humans were to be required in the future to fulfill predetermined roles in the workplace. The appropriate intelligence quotient break-point could then be determined statistically and set to deliver just the right amount of "raw material"—number of gifted students—needed to be fed into the educative processing plants and prepared to meet preset production goals. But that kind of social engineering is not overtly or covertly a part of accepted regional, national, or state planning in this country. Instead, in the United States everyone is entitled to full educational access and to equal opportunity in the workplace. Yet the intelligence quotient cut-off "identification" of gifted children practiced in the nation's schools is quite similar in style and intent to the very social engineering concept of limiting and tracking that is antithetical to the principles upon which this nation is founded. Therein lies the possible distortion of social policy suggested by a cut-off line. In summary, such "identification" is out of touch with reality and is philosophically repugnant.

BUILDING AND MAINTAINING A STEREOTYPE

The erroneous belief that a gifted person is simply someone with a high intelligence quotient is already too prevalent. It is well established in the psychoeducational literature that gifted individuals are not well described by their intelligence quotients alone (Taylor, 1969; Wallach, 1976; Freeman, 1979). It is a disservice to those who are highly capable, a twisting of reality, and an unjustifiable over-simplification to employ the intelligence quotient as the "identifier" that opens the door to special educational opportunities. Yet that practice is encouraged when "identification" is given separate status as an activity to be performed first and foremost, before anything else may be done. It reinforces the unwarranted stereotype that the high intelligence quotient defines—even constitutes—giftedness. Moreover, the authority and last word on "identification" is too frequently put in the hands of a corps of school psychologists who, because they have little or no linkage with or responsibility for the subsequent actual instruction of the "identified" pupils, also have no strong reason to attend to pupil factors such as motivation, interest, and personality variables that become progressively more influential in terms of behavioral outcomes (Ward, 1975). In consequence, the prevailing "high intelligence quotient" standard that has become the final criterion for "identification" buttresses the all-too-common stereotypic thinking about giftedness. It strengthens the mistaken notion that all gifted students are alike and reinforces the fallacious concept that, since they are all alike, one program fits all equally well.

School psychologists are capable of much more than "identification" of this sort and should not be channelled into that relatively useless activity (Trachtman, 1981). Instead they should be encouraged to engage in broad-ranging assessment of gifted children, beginning in the pre-school years.

NARROW IDENTIFICATION LEADS TO NARROW EDUCATION

"Identification" usually provides school personnel with a label to affix to the child. The label permits the educator automatically to enroll the "identified" child in a pre-existing class that is thought to be appropriate to meet the needs of children of that particular "type." Such a "typing" process, once systematized and entrenched in practice, can be a powerful deterrent and strong barrier to the recognition of the varied individual characteristics of each gifted child, the features and attributes that should guide educational interpretations and adaptations.

When teachers, psychologists and administrators focus on establishing the "identity" of a child as being gifted, they are more likely to attend only to those factors that are thought to be fairly universal and standard in their effects. If interest is in "identification," it is likely that measurement instruments, techniques, and standards almost identical for each child will be used. (That is sometimes rationalized as being in the interest of "fairness" on the part of the gatekeepers.) It is less likely, in any event, that anyone will feel motivated to explore the broader context within which the child functions and which includes social, personal, and cultural factors which contribute much to the shaping of academic abilities, limitations, special interests, and potentials. Without proper consideration of these influential forces, the persons preoccupied with "identification" can easily fail to recognize and react constructively to the child's individual strengths and weaknesses, the very qualities that make individualized special education a necessity for exceptional children.

INCREASING THE CONTRIBUTION OF SCHOOL PSYCHOLOGISTS

Twenty-five years ago Carl Pegnato discussed with me an idea for a dissertation he was planning. Out of that came a very widely cited article that introduced the "efficiency/effectiveness" concept into the process of locating gifted children and presented data in support of the concept (Pegnato & Birch, 1959). At that time, I think we both felt sure that it would not be long before all children would be examined routinely by psychologists during the year before they were scheduled to start kindergarten or first grade. In fact, demonstrations of how that might work were undertaken by us and other colleagues. Ours were based on the early school admission theme, but actually encompassing the potential to provide individual psychological examinations for all children in the community whose parents requested it while the children were between three-and-a-half and four-and-a-half years old (Sellin & Birch, 1980). Others have gone further with the concept (Pierson, 1974). Such preschool examinations, available to all children, would have a number of salutory effects, all in the direction of getting children off to a good start. Results of such assessments do give notice and time for schools to arrange accommodations that individual children are then known to need. Teachers can be ready on the day the children arrive at the door of the school.

Despite the fact that preschool psychological assessment has not caught on as a standard procedure, its potential merit is still great. The possible value has been enhanced by the increased capability of psychologists to discover potential difficulties and to arrange for the school situation to be adjusted and adapted, so that the anticipation of difficulty prevents its actual occurrence. It is essential, however, that the preschool assessment go on, hand-in-glove with the planning of individualized school programs. Otherwise, we would be right back where we are now, misusing psychologists as psychometricians and as gatekeepers (Bevan, 1981).

BEYOND THE "IDENTIFICATION → PLACEMENT" MODEL

When the "identification → placement" model prevails, the child is moved, afterward, into a "placement," which is some form of special group made up of children who have survived the same "identification" process. The intervention strategies used in that group will, ordinarily, address some global or general concepts of what gifted children are presumed to need to learn. Little attention will be paid to the need to design educational programs for each child based on individual abilities, on remediable shortcomings, or on strongly motivating enthusiasms. A "program for the gifted" placement is, because of the identification → placement model, too often encouraged to be a "set piece" for all the "identified" gifted. The model does not encourage teachers to pay attention to the possible inadequacies of instruction or content in the "set piece" for the children who are "placed" in it. The children either fit in or drop out, actually or in spirit. True enough, many or even most gifted children work with a will in such "ready-made" programs. These programs often offer some relief from an even less desirable daily routine and they supply participants with the company of other highly able companions. The "placed" children, too, have no way of knowing that what they are receiving from school may be less than it could or should be because they have had no experience with individualized education based upon their own personal patterns of potentials and past performances.

Until "identification" is replaced by psychoeducational assessment for the purpose of designing individual educational programs, it seems unlikely that much further progress will be made in education for gifted children. Fortunately, there are models that depart from the widely used "identification →placement" paradigm. Emerging models of a superior kind move in the direction of a feed-back system that has the following steps:

1. Assess abilities and interests and potentialities.

2. Design individual program of content and instructional style.

3. Implement program toward specific objectives.

4. Evaluate progress and make in-process corrections as needed.

5. Accomplish objectives.

6. Reassess abilities, interests, and potentials and repeat the process (Renzulli, 1977; Renzulli, Ries, & Smith, 1981; Sellin & Birch, 1980, 1981).

Models like these, if widely disseminated, could sharply increase the quality of psychological services and special education for gifted children and replace the "identification → placement" model.

JUSTIFIABLE IDENTIFICATION FOR STRUCTURED PROGRAMS

There are situations that properly call for narrow, tightly-constricted forms of "identification." The more structured and "group-prescribed" a special program for gifted children is, the more it may truly require some form of precise, prior "identification" for admission. If one mounts a special project solely for young people with extraordinary mathematical ability and interest, then it is eminently reasonable literally to "identify" such exceptional persons (Stanley, 1976). Likewise, were one to seek candidates for advanced instruction in the graphic arts, a particular identification procedure would make sense. Similarly, if theatrical performances or dance constituted the content of the program, particular backgrounds and interests would be sought in the candidates. There is a place for the "identification → placement" paradigm: it is particularly appropriate for focused, group-prescribed situations. It is clear, however, that in such instances the "identification" procedures and criteria are tightly program-connected. That makes it possible to view these as special cases within the broader "assess ↔ educate model."

ACCOMMODATING GIFTED CHILDREN THROUGH INDIVIDUALIZED ADAPTIVE EDUCATION

The more personalized education is, the less need there is for formal "identification." When individualized, adaptive models of instruction are the mode, gifted children, and all other children, receive the kind of education that optimizes their opportunities. By definition, adaptive education matches the content, the pace, and the teaching style of education to each child's interests, abilities, and potentials.

Individualized education does not necessarily mean "one-on-one" teaching. Rather, children sometimes work in small groups, sometimes in large groups, and sometimes individually, varying activities throughout the day. An integral part of the Adaptive Learning Environment Model (Wang & Lindvall, in press), for example, is the deliberate teaching of self-management skills to all pupils. Another integral part is the inclusion in the curriculum of a rich variety of resources for both acceleration of skill development and for the expansion of access to content areas. Moreover, for those who would emphasize "process" or "learning style," the recognized plans for individualized adaptive education tend to encourage and show teachers how to call upon higher thought processes in assigning and in questioning. They illustrate ways to make adjustments to pupil learning styles.

If one compares and contrasts the educational activities characteristic of special programs for gifted students, particularly at the primary and intermediate grade levels, with the educational characteristics of established individually adaptive education programs for all children at those levels, it is very difficult to find any important substantive or methodological differences between the two. The difference that may appear is mainly in where instruction for gifted pupils is delivered, in or out of the regular class. Gifted children in individualized, adaptive education settings do not need a separate scheme of "identification." They can be recognized by the amount, the level, and the quality of their academic and special subject attainment. Their identification is curriculum-imbedded, with regular assessment that guides and optimizes their opportunities. Special programming is open to all high potential children, not just those who first jumped the questionably relevant hurdle of an arbitrary intelligence quotient. When individualized, adaptive education is employed, starting when the gifted child begins school, curriculum-based assessment makes the older form of referral and "identification" by intelligence test scores unnecessary (Wang & Birch, 1984).

PRINCIPLES FOR SCHOOL DISTRICTS REGARDING IDENTIFICATION POLICIES AND PRACTICES

It will take time plus deliberate efforts by local school personnel to move beyond the present "identification" format in the education of gifted students.

A particular difficulty will be to dissociate special funding from the identity-label, which has encouraged the usual "identification" approach. The following principles may be helpful in bringing about the needed changes.

1. *Work toward the capability of providing full psychoeducational assessment of all children prior to school entry.* The core idea is not so much to *find* problems, but rather to *prevent* them. That is done by planning ahead to arrange kindergarten and primary grade accommodations for children who are known, as a result of preschool assessment, to need educational adaptations. Use a team of professionals, mainly kindergarten and primary teachers and school psychologists, to assess and plan for each child. If *all* children cannot be provided preschool assessment now, start by advertising and doing it at parental request, on a first-come, first-served basis, for as many children resources allow you to handle.

2. *Link all assessment of children to the same purpose, namely to plan and conduct education in terms of the needs and interests of the children.* Emphasize that all children need, for example, to learn to read, to learn mathematics, to learn history, but that the pace and breadth and style of their learning is naturally very varied. The purpose of assessment, therefore, is to give guidance regarding such matters as pace, breadth, and style of learning. The question should not be whether a child is gifted, but rather, what kinds of instructional and curricular adaptations should be arranged for the gifted child.

3. *Keep alert for gifted children who show their capabilities through school achievement, from kindergarten through 12th grade.* Encourage teachers and principals to watch for high achieving children in order to be sure that those pupils are receiving an adapted education that continues to encourage them; challenge them, and capitalize on their interests. Remember, the main function of intelligence tests, in the gifted child context, is to predict the potential for high achievement. If high achievement is already demonstrated, one doesn't need to give an intelligence test to predict it.

4. *Instruct parents, teachers, principals, librarians, physicians, counselors, supervisors, and other significant adults in what to look for to help them spot gifted children and youth at home, in school and in the community.* There are lots of useful outlines and checklists that can assist individuals to become more keen and astute observers of the various qualities of giftedness. It is possible markedly to improve both professional and lay persons' skills in childwatching. Evidence from thoughtful and concerned observers can be highly valuable in planning educational adaptations (Renzulli, Smith, White, Callahan, & Hartman, 1976).

5. *Avoid simplistic, narrow, one-dimensional approaches (like some minimum intelligence test score), even though a state or regional education agency seems to encourage it, because such approaches are both educationally unsound and politically dangerous.* It is advisable to argue, using expert opinion and public/political weaponry, with education agencies which attempt to control fund allocations by requiring compliance with unsound rules or criteria. It is better to advocate

a sound program that has solid local support than to fight local parents and friends in behalf of objectionable identification practices that invite ultimate judicial and political reversal.

SUMMARY

"Identification" of gifted students, as generally practiced in the United States, is neither desirable nor necessary. Available models of adaptive, individualized education offer alternatives more compatible philosophically and more profitable and appealing educationally. Maddux (1983), while criticizing certain views of identification, pointed out that some progress toward educational individualization can be seen, particularly with gifted students, although there still is a tendency to teach all children ". . . the same things, in the same ways, for the same period of time. If individualization of instruction were a reality, each child would receive the instruction he is ready to profit from" (p. 17). Where adaptive, individualized education is in operation, the prevailing contemporary style of "identification" no longer is needed. The replacement process should be encouraged by altered funding patterns and by leadership initiative.

REFERENCES

Bevan, W. On coming of age among the professions. In J. E. Ysseldyke, & R. A. Weinberg (Eds.), The future of psychology in the schools: Proceedings of the Spring Hill symposium. *The School Psychology Review*, 1981, *10* (2), 127–137.

Freeman, J. *Gifted children*. Baltimore: University Park, 1979.

Kirschenbaum, R. J. Let's cut out the cut-off score in the identification of the gifted. *Roeper Review*, 1983, *5* (4), 6–10.

Maddux, C. D. Early school entry for the gifted: New evidence and concerns. *Roeper Review*, 1983, *May*, 15–17.

Newland, T. E. *The gifted in socio-educational perspective*. Englewood Cliffs, NJ: Prentice-Hall, 1976.

Pegnato, C. W., & Birch, J. W. Locating gifted children in junior high school: A comparison of methods. *Exceptional Children*, 1959, *25*, 300–304.

Pierson, D. E. The Brookline early education project: Model for a new education priority. *Childhood Education*, 1974, *50* (3), 132–134.

Renzulli, J. S. *The enrichment triad model: A guide for developing defensible programs for the gifted and talented*. Mansfield Center, CT: Creative Learning Press, 1977.

Renzulli, J. S., Smith, L. H., White, A. J., Callahan, C. M., & Hartman, R. K. *Scales for rating the behavioral characteristics of superior students*. Mansfield Center, CT: Creative Learning Press, 1976.

Renzulli, J. S., Reis, S. M., & Smith, L. H. *The revolving door identification model*. Mansfield Center, CT: Creative Learning Press, 1981.

Reynolds, M. C. (Ed.). Futures of education for exceptional students. Reston, VA: The Council for Exceptional Children, 1978.

Sellin, D. E., & Birch, J. W. *Education of gifted and talented learners.* Rockville, MD: Aspen Systems, 1980.

Sellin, D. E., & Birch, J. W. *Psychoeducational development of gifted and talented learners.* Rockville, MD: Aspen Systems, 1981.

Sellin, D. E., & Birch, J. W. *Educating gifted and talented learners.* Rockville, MD: Aspen Systems, 1980.

Stanley, J. Identifying and nurturing the intellectually gifted. *Phi Delta Kappan,* 1976, *58* (6), 234–237.

Taylor, C. W. The highest potential of man. *Gifted Child Quarterly,* 1969, *2,* 9–30.

Trachtman, G. M. On such a full sea. In J. E. Ysseldyke, & R.A. Weinberg (Eds.), The future of psychology in the schools: Proceedings of the Spring Hill symposium. *The School Psychology Review,* 1981, *10* (2), 138–181.

Wallach, M. A. Creativity. In P.H. Mussen (Ed.), *Charmichael's manual of child psychology* (3rd Ed.). NYC: John Wiley, 1976.

Wang, M. C., & Birch, J. W. Comparison of a full-time mainstreaming program and a resource room approach. *Exceptional Children,* 1984, *51* (1), 33–40.

Wang, M. C., & Lindvall, C. M. Individual differences in school learning environments: Theory, research, and design. In E. W. Gordon (Ed.), *Review of research in education: Vol. II.* Washington, DC: American Educational Research Association (in press).

Ward, V. S. Basic concepts. In W. Barbe, & J. Renzulli (Eds.), *Psychology and education of the gifted.* NYC: Irvington, 1975.

2

Myth: There Must Be "Winners" and "Losers" in Identification and Programming!

Response by Carolyn M. Callahan

A most unfortunate byproduct of many current approaches to identifying and serving gifted and talented children is the perception that children are either "in" the program (THE WINNERS) or they are "not in" the program (THE LOSERS). Associated with the status of WINNER are the positive advantages of the label of gifted, the opportunity for special activities, access to new resources and challenges, and often a chance to escape the tedium of the regular classroom. To the LOSERS go the feelings of inadequacy, the feelings of being left out, and the disappointments of not meeting parental expectations. These perceptions and feelings (whether justified or not) certainly contribute to the negative charges that gifted programs are elitist and exclusive. It is hard to deny

Editor's Note: From Callahan, C. M. (1982). Myth: There must be "winners" and "losers" in identification and programming! *Gifted Child Quarterly, 26*(1), 17-19. © 1982 National Association for Gifted Children. Reprinted with permission.

exclusivity when some students are clearly denied the opportunity to participate in activities which other children have the privilege of attending. It is especially hard when these activities clearly appear to be more "fun" than the regular classroom activities. It is also hard to deny exclusivity when we present hard-line "all-or-none" programming options which separate all "activities for the gifted" from the mainstream of education.

Some have chosen to counter these charges with the retort that it is the right rather than the privilege of the gifted child to receive a differentiated curriculum. The right to a differentiated curriculum cannot be denied. However, does such a right also give these children exclusive access to activities which might also be of benefit to other children? Do gifted children alone need to develop creative thinking or critical thinking skills? And does the concept of differentiated curriculum suggest (as our programs most often do) that all gifted children are the same in their needs and that no other children share some of these needs or might benefit from some of these activities at certain points in their school careers? To accept those assumptions is to deny all of the knowledge we have about the growth, development, and learning of children.

All myths evolve from some set of beliefs or some interpretation of unexplainable phenomena, and some looking at the sources of myths can help debunk the myth. Although we can never be sure of the origins of a myth, we can speculate that this particular myth has evolved through a distortion of some fundamentally sound and widely-accepted axioms in gifted education. For example, one potential source of this myth is the demand that we have "identifiable" programs for the gifted. This axiom has been translated to mean that the program must have one or more of the following attributes: a "gifted teacher," a resource source room, a specific time when the program is offered, and/or a specific group of children known as "the gifted." This interpretation is not only dangerous in that it contributes to the perpetuation of the myth of exclusivity, it also shortchanges the gifted child. Having a gifted teacher who works in a resource room using special materials for some specified period of time limits the potential for total curriculum planning for the gifted child; it allows the regular classroom teacher to assume that the "giftedness" of the child is "taken care of" in the resource room; and allows us to let children with special learning needs who have not yet been identified for the special program to vegetate while they wait. It also contributes to the narrowness of services offered by most school divisions. When we cannot afford to have special resource rooms or special teachers for the intellectually gifted, the mathematically gifted, the artistically talented, etc., we then severely restrict our definition in order to accommodate only some small portion of the total gifted population.

Before the reader draws the conclusion that the resources mentioned above are not desirable, it should be pointed out that these resources are both desirable and clearly necessary for total programming; however they are usually not sufficient for total programming for gifted children. Furthermore, expanding the conception of programming does not suggest that all children are gifted. It is also not meant to suggest that there will never be occasions when some children will need the opportunity to meet with highly trained and specialized teachers; nor does it imply that a gifted child does not need special instruction and special materials. Rather, it is meant to imply that we should consider the total educational program of the gifted child and all other children and plan for the special needs of those children regardless of the setting or the instructor. When any child has a need that can be met through the use of a given set of resources, then he or she should have access to the resources. And that access should be based on "action" information on the child rather than the static information provided by three-year-old test scores (Renzulli, 1981). Under such conditions there need not be winners or losers but only students engaged in differing learning experiences in a variety of settings according to level of ability and achievements, interests, and learning styles.

The second axiom contributing to the myth is that gifted children must be identified (through a defensible identification process) in order to be served. This seemingly innocuous and completely rational statement often leads to a corollary: All gifted students must be labelled (or more fashionably "tagged") before their needs can be met or before they are entitled to receive services. Note the subtle difference between the axiom and the corollary. The axiom suggests that we must look for those characteristics which differentiate the gifted child from other children and then plan educational programs to meet the needs which emanate from these characteristics. All that is well and good! However, the corollary suggests that we must label these children *before* they can rightfully expect to receive any kind of services. It seems as if the purpose of labelling takes precedence in the identification process. Because of the sensitivity that results from such an exclusionary labelling process, in some school divisions there is considerably more emphasis on planning for this identification process than on planning for strategies to program for the children. When such importance is placed on the identification process, the parents often expend considerable effort in assuring that the child receives the label rather than focusing on what is offered to the child as a result.

The label is, of course, convenient. It allows us to disregard providing services to any child who doesn't measure up to *our* criteria or definition. For example, consider a child from a school division which places in the gifted program only those children who are in the top 5% according to total scores on a matrix. A child who scores in the 99th percentile in achievement in mathematics and who is very capable of doing work many grade levels above current placement in mathematics *but* who does not score exceptionally high in any other area is not likely to be "identified." And he/she is also not likely to have special provisions made in his/her mathematics program.

Given the imperfections in our traditional identification procedures (consider the number of gifted adults who never would have been identified as gifted children) and the fact that children are considered "gifted" in one school division and "not gifted" in another school division, the belief that the only children who have needs for a different curriculum are those who happen to fit our particular definition of giftedness and meet our particular standards of "admission" seems narrow and unjustified. Doesn't it seem more appropriate to focus the identification process on searching for those children whose exceptional ability warrants modifications in their school curriculum and then provide the appropriate modification through whatever resources (including teachers, materials, scheduling, etc.) are needed? Identification then becomes defensible on the grounds that children who require a differentiated program are provided with that program. That reduces the need to label children and increases the attention given to programming.

A third and related source of the forced categorization of students are the formulas and guidelines set out by funding agencies. State funding formulas necessarily limit the number or percentage of children in a school division for whom special monies will be provided. They also require the school divisions to identify these specific children who are being served. Unfortunately, the school division often interprets such guidelines in the most limiting of all possible ways and presumes that only those children who have been "named" can receive those services paid for by the "gifted money." In one school division books and materials in the professional library were labelled "FOR USE BY THE GIFTED TEACHERS ONLY." A more appropriate expenditure of these monies is to assure that there is a conscious systematic effort to identify *all* exceptionally talented and advanced children in the school division and provide appropriate educational programs as those programs are warranted. For some students this may mean a differentiated curriculum across all subject areas, for others this may mean special services in only mathematics or music or science. For some students these curricular modifications may be handled by regular classroom teachers and in other cases there will be a need for special resource rooms, materials, and personnel. To the extent that "money for the gifted" is perceived as part of the process of providing a challenging educational program and expanding/supplementing the regular curriculum as warranted by current levels of functioning, there will be a decreased tendency to perceive gifted programs as providing special favors to an exclusive few.

Finally, the absurdities and cruelties which are perpetuated by the myth and the associated labels are the most serious of concerns. One of these is the eternal question of why a child is "gifted" in one school division and all of a sudden "not gifted" when moved to another school division. The dilemma results from the importance attached to the label rather than to attention to the curriculum offered to the child in the classroom and judging the resulting need for differentiation. One state legislature even determined that there were "too many" gifted children in the state and sought to raise the criteria for "giftedness" by establishing an IQ of 140 as a cut-off to replace the former criteria of 130. This action would have resulted in the creation of a whole new category of children whom we could label "the formerly gifted." One expert in the field has likened this to an ailing patient appearing at the physician's office with a temperature of 105° and being told, "I'm sorry but you're not really sick. We've been having too many patients with fevers of 105° so we've raised the criteria for sickness to 107°."

The key issue is not whether a child is gifted or not gifted. Those labels are useful to us only in the sense that they (a) create an awareness that there exists a population of students whose exceptional abilities differentiate them from the rest of the student population and (b) suggest some characteristics which we should attend to in planning educational programs for those children. The label is also important in gaining recognition that these modifications may require additional expenditure of funds to train teachers in meeting the gifted child's needs, in providing special teachers as necessary, for additional materials, etc. From that point on, the issue of education of the gifted should revolve around the degree to which any child's needs are being met through the regular curriculum, the degree to which the curriculum should be enriched and/or accelerated, and who will be responsible for that modification in the program.

REFERENCE

Renzulli, J. S., Reis, S. M., & Smith, L. H. *Revolving door identification model.* Mansfield Center, CT: Creative Learning Press, 1981.

3

The Role of Creativity in Identification of the Gifted and Talented

E. Paul Torrance

For more than 40 years I have maintained that creativity should always be one of the criteria considered in identifying gifted and talented students. I welcome this opportunity to review briefly some of the events that led me to this conclusion and have continued to reinforce it and to restate what I regard as the most important principles that should guide school systems in their identification policies and procedures.

THE PROBLEM

Throughout history, a common characteristic of those who have made outstanding artistic and scientific contributions, social improvements, technological

Editor's Note: From Torrance, E. P. (1984). The role of creativity in identification of the gifted and talented. *Gifted Child Quarterly, 28*(4), 153–156. © 1984 National Association for Gifted Children. Reprinted with permission.

breakthroughs, and the like has been their creativity. The importance of identifying and developing creative talent has been argued by historians such as Toynbee (1964), futurists (Polak, 1973), scientists (Seaborg, 1963), educators (Torrance, 1979). Today there are additional reasons why it is necessary to give a fair chance to creative children, young people, and adults. We are living in an age of increasing rates of change, depleted natural resources, threats of nuclear war, interdependence, and destandardization. All of these forces require us to utilize increased ingenuity and creativity.

These matters are widely acknowledged facts, yet legislators, educational leaders, and even scholars of gifted education express a peculiar ambivalence about using creativity as a criterion in identifying gifted and talented students and applying the technology we have developed to facilitate this process and the development and improvement of creative functioning.

For centuries, Buddhists have used a kind of creativity test *(koans)* to select gifted candidates for training. The ancient Chinese and Japanese identified their geniuses by having them create poems on such topics as plum blossoms in the moonlight. Although Western societies have been generally ambivalent and often opposed to identifying and deliberately developing creative talent, patrons and sponsors in the Golden Ages of creative achievement in Italy, Greece, and France did it.

Perhaps the most difficult and fundamental problem in identifying creatively gifted and talented children is that of dealing with a national climate that is generally unfavorable to creative achievement. This is further complicated by a national climate that rather generally discourages the full development of potentialities, except for certain types of athletics. The problem is especially severe in the South. This problem was described rather eloquently some years ago by Lillian Smith (1949) in *Killers of the Dream.* She pointed out such paradoxes as the fact that we value beautiful things but import them from Asia and Europe to derogate our native sons who aspire to create beautiful things. We have feared hands that create but have accepted and honored hands that destroyed. In the South, as perhaps nowhere else, creativity has been considered sinful. We went through a long period in which the new learning, science, was considered sinful. I grew up in Georgia in such an environment. I can recall vividly, when I was thinking of going to college and hopelessly searching for the resources to do so, many of my friends were afraid that I would be exposed to this sinful science. Curiosity was sinful. Humor was sinful. Dancing was sinful. *Anything* creative was sinful.

This paradox, however, is not limited to the South, the creation of beautiful things, or to the time prior to 1957. Even now in these times of economic crisis, our inventors and researchers are treated rather shabbily and many of our corporations prefer to purchase high technology from Japan or Germany rather than permit our inventors and researchers to develop their own. As a consequence the number of patents and inventions by citizens of the United States has been dropping since 1978. Since 1967, Japan has been increasing its lead over the United States in the number of patents and inventions each year

(Orkin, 1974). Orkin (1981) and others attribute this lag to laws that do not protect the rights of inventors and rob them of their just rewards.

MY PERSONAL ODYSSEY

When I began teaching eighth and ninth graders in 1936 after completing only two years of college, I wondered why I had so much trouble with a few creatively gifted students I tried to teach. (There was no problem of identification. Their creativity was richly manifest in the thousands of strategies they invented to defeat me.) I punished them and punished them, about the only thing that I knew then to do. This bothered me, as I knew they were gifted and that I was not able to meet their needs. (Incidentally, these creatively gifted troublemakers later became school superintendents, labor negotiators, ministers, and one of them Secretary of Labor in the Ford Presidential Cabinet.)

My problem became even more severe during my second year of teaching at Georgia Military College High School, a local high school for boys and a boarding school primarily for boys who were unable to adapt to their local high schools. Generally, their creative giftedness was at the seat of their behavior and learning problems. Somehow, I developed some teaching strategies and methods that worked. I was especially successful in teaching students who failed certain courses like geometry during the first semester. I taught them for the second semester, and generally most of them outachieved their classmates in the original classes who had passed the first semester. When I began teaching these special classes, my teaching colleagues pitied me for being assigned so many "unteachable" students. However, they became angry when my students outachieved their own at the end of the year on standardized achievement tests. Somehow, I had been able to use the creative strengths of these students and they had overcome unfavorable attitudes about the subject matter, learning more in one semester than their peers had learned in two semesters.

It was during this period that I developed in 1943 my first creativity test. By that time, I had become involved in counselor training, tests and measurements, and the like. It seemed to me that the available tests did not identify the kinds of giftedness that I sensed in so many of my students.

This work was interrupted in 1945 by my military service in World War II, counseling disabled veterans following World War II, studying how to train aircrews to survive emergencies and extreme conditions, and trying to find out what made some fighter pilots aces. My military assignment in World War II was to interview and prepare classification summaries for men who had been courtmartialed and later to develop a program to prepare them to re-enter life outside of prison. Again, it was clear to me that many of these men were in trouble on account of their creativity and that their successful adaptation to society would depend upon their management of this creativity. Many times, I was painfully aware that a lack of measure of creative talent made it difficult for me to support adequately a disabled veteran's plans for the future. As I began to study the psychology of survival in emergencies and extreme conditions, it soon became clear to me that training for survival should include training in creative problem solving. Thus, many of the assessment instruments we developed and the training procedures we suggested revolved around this insight. As my associates and I completed our intensive personality studies of the United States jet aces in Korea, it also became clear that a distinguishing characteristic of these aces was their creativity.

When I became director of the Bureau of Educational Research at the University of Minnesota in 1958, the advisory committee recommended that we initiate a pioneering program of research on giftedness. College of Education Dean Walter W. Cook was firmly committed to the concept of a variety of kinds of giftedness and the advisory committee was approving. It was then easy for me to make the decision to begin work on the identification of creatively gifted and talented students and the cultivation of this kind of giftedness.

DEVELOPMENT OF TESTS OF CREATIVE TALENT

My research assistants and I began work almost immediately with students at all educational levels. I had been taught that almost all scientific progress is dependent upon the development and calibration of instruments for measuring the phenomena under investigation. We developed a variety of tests of creative thinking ability, creative motivation scales, and biographical inventories based upon our theories about the life experiences through which creative thinking skills and creative motivations and commitment develop. Most of our predictive validity studies, however, were targeted to test the validity of a general purpose battery of creative thinking ability tests that could be used from kindergarten through graduate and professional education.

Our first major predictive validity study (Torrance, Tan, & Allman, 1970) was with elementary education majors who were followed up eight years later. Tan and I developed a checklist of creative behavior exhibited by elementary teachers and this yielded a measure of creative behavior for 114 of the subjects who had become elementary school teachers and returned our follow-up questionnaire. Coefficients of correlation of .62 and .57 were obtained between the indices of creative teaching behavior and two measures of verbal creativity obtained at the time they were juniors in elementary education.

At the same time I initiated the elementary teacher study, I also began longitudinal studies with both elementary and high school students. The high school students were followed up in 1970 (Torrance, 1972), 12 years later, and the elementary school students were followed up in 1980 (Torrance, 1981), 22 years later. In my opinion, both of these studies have yielded encouraging results and have shown clear relationships between creativity test performances in elementary and high school and "real life" creative achievements.

In the high school study, follow-up data were obtained from 230 subjects. These data included: information about publicly recognized and acknowledged creative achievements (such as patents and inventions, new products developed and marketed, books published, scientific discoveries, awards in the arts and sciences, new businesses initiated, and the like); descriptions of their three highest creative achievements; and future career images. An overall validity coefficient of .51 was obtained for the creativity measures and these criteria. For males, this validity coefficient was .59 and for females it was .46 (Torrance, 1972).

In the elementary school study, follow-up data were obtained for 220 subjects. The same kinds of follow-up data were obtained for them as had been obtained for their older counterparts. In addition, data were obtained about their more personal, not publicly recognized, creative achievements. Even though this study covered a span of 22 years, the validity coefficients were equally as good as in the 12-year study. For males, the overall validity coefficient was .62; for females, it was .57. For the total sample, an overall validity coefficient of .63 was obtained. Although the creativity test predictors leave considerable unexplained variance, it is unusual to find higher predictive validity for intelligence and achievement tests or other predictor variables in similar studies. In the present study, validity coefficients for measures of intelligence ranged from −.02 to .34 and averaged .17. In the present study, it was found that additional variance could be explained by such things as having certain teachers known for encouraging creativity, having a mentor, having a future career image during the elementary school years, and having experiences with foreign study and living. Thus, I believe that the predictive validity is as good as we have any right to expect for almost any kind of predictor of adult achievements (Torrance, 1981).

Although there have been several predictive validity studies with the *Torrance Tests of Creative Thinking*, as well as with other creativity predictors, except for two by Howieson (1981, 1984), all of them have been for relatively short periods (usually about five years). Howieson (1981) reported a 10-year follow-up study covering the period from 1965 to 1975 in Australia. Her subjects were 400 seventh graders and the criterion data consisted of responses to the Wallach and Wing (1969) checklist of creative achievements outside of the school curriculum. The total score on the *Torrance Tests of Creative Thinking* correlated .30 with the total criterion score. As in the Torrance studies, the predictions were more accurate for the males than for the females. Howieson (1984) has just completed a 23-year follow-up study using predictor data collected in 1960 by Torrance in Western Australia. Although the verbal measures derived from the *Torrance Tests of Creative Thinking* failed to predict adult creative achievements at a satisfactory level for the 306 subjects who returned their questionnaires, the figural measures fared rather well. For her measure of quality of publicly recognized creative achievements, Howieson obtained a multiple correlation coefficient of .51; for quantity of personal (not publicly recognized) creative achievements, a multiple coefficient of correlation of .33; and for quality of personal creative achievements, one of .44.

It is not possible to estimate accurately the extent to which creativity tests are now being used to identify the gifted and talented. Yarborough and Johnson (1983) reported a survey of 36 state departments of education which resulted in the identification of 109 outstanding programs for the gifted and talented. In 31% of the 87 programs supplying appropriate data, creativity tests had been used in identification. In some states, creativity tests are listed among the acceptable criteria for identifying the gifted; in some, creativity tests are not mentioned as acceptable criteria; and in still others, creativity tests are explicitly named as unacceptable criteria. In most instances, the *Torrance Tests of Creative Thinking* and other measures of creative talent are used as a part of multiple criteria selection, employing some device such as the *Baldwin Identification Matrix* (Baldwin & Wooster, 1977) wherein several indicators of giftedness are weighted and a composite index developed. In some instances, a group intelligence test is used for initial screening and a creativity test is administered to students who attain a certain cut-off score (such as an IQ of 115 or higher) but do not achieve a higher cut-off score such as 130, 135, or 140.

Documentation of Validity of Creativity as a Criterion

Students in the IQ range of 115 to 130 who are identified as creatively gifted (generally Creativity Indices of 130 or higher) seem to hold their own quite well in academically-oriented gifted programs and achieve as well as their less creative peers who have IQs of 130 or higher. In defending this position, I have cited my earlier studies (Torrance, 1962) and the Getzels and Jackson (1962) study which showed that creatively gifted students missing such cut-off points as 130 IQs, achieve as well as their classmates with IQs in excess of 130 who would be classified as creatively gifted by similar standards.

More convincing, however, is my comparative longitudinal study of the adult creative achievements of elementary school children identified as highly intelligent and highly creative (Torrance and Wu, 1981). On all four of the criteria of adult creative achievement (number of publicly recognized creative achievements, number of personal creative achievements, quality of highest creative achievements, and quality of future career images), the highly creative group excelled over the highly intelligent group and equaled those who were highly intelligent and highly creative. They also achieved as many post high-school degrees, honors, and other academic attainments as their more intelligent (higher IQ) counterparts.

RECOMMENDED PRINCIPLES
FOR IDENTIFICATION POLICIES AND PROCEDURES

In summary, I suggest the following five policies and procedures regarding the identification of the gifted and the talented on the basis of the experiences and research described herein:

1. Creativity should almost always be one of the criteria, though not the sole criterion. In general, when creativity indicators are used, students who might otherwise be missed, should be included rather than to exclude anyone.

2. Different kinds of excellence (multiple talents) should be evaluated. Society needs many different kinds of talent and schools should encourage them.

3. Where disabilities and sensory handicaps are involved and where young children (3 to 6 years) are involved, attention must be given to procedures that permit responses in a modality possible for the student.

4. Where disadvantaged and culturally different children are involved, attention must also be given to the selection of test tasks that assess the kinds of excellence that are valued in the particular culture or subculture of the children being evaluated.

5. Even in using creativity tests, select one that considers a wide variety of indicators rather than a single one. For example, the new streamlined scoring of the figural forms of the *Torrance Tests of Creative Thinking* (Torrance & Ball, 1984; Howieson, 1984) which considers five norm-referenced and thirteen criterion-referenced indicators, yields better predictive validity than does the earlier scoring system which considers only four norm-referenced indicators.

REFERENCES

Baldwin, A. Y., & Wooster, J. *Baldwin identification matrix inservice kit for the identification of gifted and talented students.* Buffalo, NY: DOK Publishers, 1977.

Getzels, J. W., & Jackson, P. W. *Creativity and intelligence.* NYC: John Wiley, 1962.

Howieson, N. A longitudinal study of creativity: 1965–1975. *Journal of Creative Behavior,* 1981, *15,* 117–135.

Howieson, N. The prediction of creative achievement from childhood measures: A longitudinal study in Australia, 1960–1983. Unpublished doctoral dissertation, University of Georgia, 1984.

Orkin, N. Legal rights of the employed inventor: New approaches to old problems. *Journal of the Patent Office Society,* 1974, December.

Orkin, H. The legal rights of the employed inventor in the United States: A labor-management perspective. In J. Phillips (Ed.), Employees' inventions: *A comparative study.* Sunderland, England: Fernsway Publications, 1981.

Polak, F. L. *The image of the future.* NYC: Elsevier, 1973.

Seaborg, G. T. Training the creative scientist. *Science Newsletter,* 1963, *83,* 314.

Smith, L. *Killers of the dream.* NYC: Norton, 1949.

Torrance, E. P. *Guiding creative talent.* Englewood Cliffs, NJ: Prentice Hall, 1962.

Torrance, E. P. Career patterns and peak creative achievements of creative high school students 12 years later. *Gifted Child Quarterly,* 1972, *16,* 75–88.

Torrance, E. P. *The Torrance tests of creative thinking: Norms-technical manual.* Bensenville, IL: Scholastic Testing Service, 1974.

Torrance, E. P. *The search for satori and creativity.* Buffalo, NY: Creative Education Foundation, 1979.

Torrance, E. P. Predicting the "creativity of elementary school children (1958–80)—and the teacher who "made a difference." *Gifted Child Quarterly,* 1981, *25,* 55–62.

Torrance, E. P., & Ball, O. E. *Torrance tests of creative thinking: Streamlined (revised) manual, figural A and B.* Bensenville, IL: Scholastic Testing Service, 1984.

Torrance, E. P., Tan, C. A., & Allman, T. Verbal originality and teacher behavior: A predictive validity study. *Journal of Teacher Education*, 1970, 21, 335–341.

Torrance, E. P., & Wu, T. H. A comparative longitudinal study of the adult creative achievements of elementary school children identified as highly intelligent and as highly creative. *Creative Child and Adult Quarterly*, 1981, 6, 71–76.

Toynbee, A. Is America neglecting her creative minority? In C. W. Taylor (Ed.), *Widening horizons of creativity.* NYC: John Wiley, 1964.

Wallach, M., & Wing, C. W., Jr. *The talented student.* NYC: Holt, Rinehart & Winston, 1969.

Yarborough, B. H., & Johnson, R. A. Identifying the gifted: A theory-practice gap. *Gifted Child Quarterly*, 1983, 27, 135–138.

4

Identifying Young, Potentially Gifted, Economically Disadvantaged Students

James H. Borland

Lisa Wright

Teachers College, Columbia University

In this paper we present a rationale for and a description of the procedures developed by the staff of Project Synergy for identifying economically disadvantaged, potentially gifted kindergarten students in urban schools. This approach emphasizes the development of site-appropriate methods, observation, dynamic assessment, and the concept of best performance; it de-emphasizes the use of standardized tests. Validation data are presented and discussed.

Editor's Note: From Borland, J. H., & Wright, L. (1994). Identifying young, potentially gifted, economically disadvantaged students. *Gifted Child Quarterly*, *38*(4), 164-171. © 1994 National Association for Gifted Children. Reprinted with permission.

Numerous writers (e.g., Borland, 1989; Gallagher, 1985; Howley, Howley, & Pendarvis, 1986) have remarked upon how intractable problems associated with what Tannenbaum (1983, p. 342) calls the "inexact science" of identifying gifted students seem to be. Since giftedness is a value-laden social construct the assessment of which often involves methods and instruments of uncertain validity, it is unreasonable to expect otherwise. Identification problems will probably bedevil educators as long as there are programs for gifted students.

Some of the most persistent and troubling problems bear on the issue of equity. Ours is a multiracial, multiethnic society with marked between-group variation in the economic means available to families—and thus in the educational expectations, experiences, and attainments of their children (see. e.g., Kozol, 1991). Unfortunately, there is evidence (e.g., Passow, 1989; Richert, 1987; VanTassel-Baska, Patton, & Prillaman, 1989) that we have failed, as a field, to respond to our society's diversity by adequately identifying and serving gifted students who are economically disadvantaged, especially students from racial and ethnic minority groups.

The National Educational Longitudinal Study of eighth-grade programs for gifted students by the U.S. Department of Education (1991) reveals the extent of the problem rather dramatically. Data from the study indicate that students whose families' socioeconomic status places them in the top quartile of the population are about five times more likely to be in programs for gifted students than are students from families in the bottom quartile.

This prompts some (e.g., Myers, 1991; Slavin, 1991) to urge an end to gifted programs altogether and to argue that inequity is inherent in such programs. However, it strikes us as illogical to respond to the problem of underserved gifted students by eliminating services to those being served. Rather, we believe the rational, humane course of action is to provide appropriate educational opportunities to those now denied them, especially gifted students who are economically disadvantaged and members of racial and ethnic minority groups, the students Project Synergy was designed to serve.

Project Synergy is funded by the U.S. Department of Education as a research and development project of the Department of Special Education and the Leta Hollingworth Center at Teachers College, Columbia University, and is designed to generate new ways to identify and educate young, economically disadvantaged, potentially gifted students. The purpose of this article is to describe the identification procedures developed by the staff of Project Synergy.

WORKING PRINCIPLES

Before describing the identification process, we want to set forth the principles that guided its development.

   1. *The potential for academic giftedness is present in roughly equal proportions in all groups in our society.*

This fundamental principle motivates our efforts and underscores the extent of the problem. If this is true, we must question the skewed allocation of special educational resources for gifted students in a manner that unfairly benefits the white middle and upper classes.

2. *Gifted education is a form of special education.*

This principle, discussed elsewhere by the first author (Borland, 1989), undergirds our view of giftedness as exceptionality relative to the mean level of ability in a specific setting, here, a school in central Harlem. A special educational conception of giftedness makes applying the term *gifted* possible in a school where few students exceed the national mean on standardized measures of achievement and focuses our attention on the needs of individual students.

Putting the Research to Use

Identifying economically disadvantaged gifted students has been a difficult problem for the field since its inception. The methods described in this article point to some approaches to the problem that have some empirical support. In particular, the use of observation, portfolio assessment, dynamic assessment, and case study methods are recommended to educators for consideration and possible use in the identification of economically disadvantaged and other gifted students.

---

3. *Identifying economically, disadvantaged, potentially gifted students differs from identifying other gifted students with respect to the goal of identification.*

Placing potentially gifted economically disadvantaged students in special classes for gifted students can be problematic. The effects of poverty, racism, and class bias are real, often resulting in significant educational disadvantages (Natriello, McDill, & Pallas, 1990) for these students relative to gifted students who are not economically disadvantaged. Such placements may become sink-or-swim situations. This illustrates the need for what we call *transitional services*, interventions designed to help potentially gifted students develop their latent abilities. In Project Synergy, placement in classes for gifted students is the long-term goal; placement in transitional services is the immediate goal. We thus seek evidence of undeveloped potential, not necessarily realized ability.

4. *Knowledge needed to identify disadvantaged gifted students is to be found in school classrooms, not the research literature.*

This is true partly by default; the literature on disadvantaged gifted students is exiguous and often platitudinous. More important, every school is unique in ways that can nurture or suppress giftedness in that setting. Thus, in Project Synergy, we resisted the temptation to formulate identification procedures a priori in the hope that they would match the realities we would later encounter in the real world of the schools. Instead, we approached the school in which we worked with our eyes and minds open, bringing more questions than answers.

5. *The human being is the identification instrument of choice.*

Economically disadvantaged children face serious impediments to success in a society that is in many respects racist and has what some (e.g., Ogbu, 1978, 1992) call a caste system. Tests with predictive validity for academic achievement will necessarily reflect this, as evidenced by the gap between the mean IQs of African-American and Caucasian children (e.g., Jensen, 1980). Attempts to overcome this discrepancy by manipulating test scores (for example, by using a matrix) or creating "culture-fair" or "culture-free" tests have not been promising. The answer, we believe, is to use "the human instrument" (Lincoln & Guba, 1985, p. 39), trading the objectivity of standardized tests for the sensitivity and adaptability of human observation and judgment.

6. *The concept of "best performance" is valid in identifying giftedness in young economically disadvantaged children.*

As Roedell, Jackson, and Robinson argue,

> very young children ... rarely ... can be relied upon to demonstrate the best performance of which they are capable during all phases of a test session. ... [T]he most meaningful aspect of a young child's test performance is not the child's average level of performance across a wide range of tasks, but the most advanced performance demonstrated. (1980, p. 38)

This is even more true for young children whose intellectual and experiential stimulation has been minimal and inconsistent. Thus, for identification purposes, we look for any sign of advanced performance that might represent untapped potential. This precludes the use of a matrix or any process involving the averaging of data and requires using many varied indicators to increase the probability of uncovering an area of advanced performance or potential.

THE RESEARCH SETTING AND THE STUDENTS

The methods described below were developed at, and used to identify children attending, Public School 149/207 in central Harlem. New York City, during academic years 1990–91, 1991–92, and 1992–93. The school's student body is three-quarters African-American and one-quarter Hispanic; nearly all students are economically disadvantaged. Life in the neighborhood presents numerous challenges for parents and children. Violence is not foreign to their lives; for some it is part of family life. Drug use is widespread, barely stopping at the schoolhouse door. On one of our first visits to the school, one of the project staff mentally drew a semicircle with a 10 foot radius on the sidewalk in front of the school's front door and within that area counted over 30 discarded crack vials.

P.S. 149/207 is a School Under Registration Review; owing to low student achievement, its performance is being monitored by the state, and decertification is a possibility. In 1992–93. the school ranked 617th out of 625 New York City public elementary schools with respect to scores on the Degrees of Reading Power Test, with only 14.1% of its students on grade level. However, as the principal and teachers insist, and our experience confirms, there are children at P.S. 149/207 with the potential for academic giftedness.

THE IDENTIFICATION PROCESS

Preliminary Activities

Effective identification requires clear goals. Since our long term goal is to place identified students in programs for gifted students, our conception of giftedness focuses on the potential for high-level academic aptitude. A short-term goal is to identify 15 to 18 students annually from about 100 children in the kindergarten classes (three English, one bilingual). This is a high percentage of the school's kindergarten population, but we anticipated, correctly, that of 15 identified children, about 12 would enroll in the transitional services classes in the summer following kindergarten and that there would subsequently be attrition for various reasons.

Once these goals were established, we began spending time in the kindergartens to get a feel for the classroom culture. There were no formal observations and no systematic record keeping. We simply were there, becoming acquainted with the children and the teachers and their daily experiences, letting the teachers and children become accustomed to our presence. Once this was accomplished, the formal process of identification began. What follows is a description of the process as it has evolved over the 3 years of the project.

Phase I: Screening

The first phase of the identification process is called *screening* (see Figure 1), the goal of which is to form a candidate pool roughly two to three times larger in number than the cohort that we will ultimately identify as potentially gifted. Sources of information for screening are the following.

Nontraditional assessment: Classroom observation. We observe each kindergarten student twice as he or she engages in free play and structured academic activities. Observations last approximately 5 minutes, during which time we attempt to keep a complete running record of the child's behavior to interpret later. For rich detail and ecological validity, direct observation of student behavior is unparalleled as a means of assessment, and, as Chittenden (1991) argues, "this is potentially the richest source of information" (p. 25). Although there are certain traits—creativity, perseverance, problem solving, and so forth—to which

Figure 1   Components of Phase I of the Identification Process: Screening

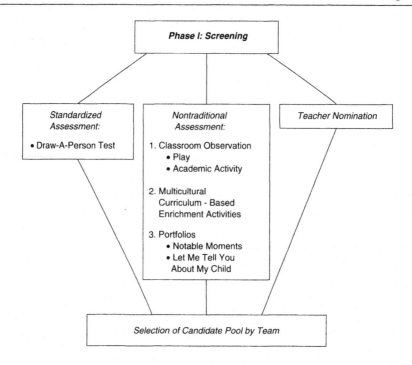

we are especially alert, we observe and record each behavior so we can reflect on it later to determine whether it suggests potential giftedness.

Nontraditional assessment: Multicultural curriculum-based enrichment activities. In this component of the screening we expose all children, in groups, to enrichment activities and observe their behavior. We read a story with African-American characters (for the bilingual class, a story in Spanish with Hispanic characters) and then have the children engage in art, language, and mathematics activities. We record children's behavior during the story and the follow-up activities and place the resulting products in the students' files. This activity serves two additional purposes: (a) it provides inservice education in curriculum differentiation to teachers, and (b) it focuses the teachers' attention on behaviors that might not have been elicited by previous classroom activities, which is useful when teachers nominate students for the candidate pool (see below).

Standardized assessment: Draw-a-person test. Figure drawing tests have many applications, projective as well as cognitive. We use such a test for the latter purpose in Project Synergy and assess the results according to developmental levels of drawing (Harris, 1963). In addition, this gives us some insight into figural creativity.

Portfolio assessment. Following a procedure developed by the second author and implemented and tested in other settings, kindergarten teachers at P.S. 149/207 use early childhood developmental portfolios to gather information about and gain insight into the progress of their students (see Wright & Borland, 1993). The portfolios provide a practical means for regular classroom teachers to observe, record, and store examples of students' work and behavior.

"Let-Me-Tell-You-About-My-Child" cards, in English and Spanish, are a part of the portfolio that kindergarten teachers send home with the children. In a letter, the teacher asks the parents to list on one or more cards anything their child does at home that reflects the child's abilities or interests. Although parents have knowledge about children to which no one else is privy, obtaining this knowledge can be difficult. Some parents are illiterate, limited in English proficiency, suspicious of school personnel, or absent from the home. Others have problems—including drug, alcohol, emotional, immigration, or other difficulties—that compromise their ability and willingness to cooperate with school authorities. However, the "Let-Me-Tell-You-About-My-Child" cards have yielded useful identification information, and we hope that as the portfolios become more a part of the classroom routine, parents will become more productive sources of information.

"Notable Moment Cards," another component of the portfolios, allow teachers to document children's activities or accomplishments of special note, reinforcing the teachers' role as observer and identifier of potential giftedness. The cards go into the portfolios and become part of the information available for identification.

Teacher nomination. Teachers are asked to nominate children for the candidate pool. We do not use a checklist since we believe their use restricts teachers' attention to a limited realm of predetermined traits and behaviors. We are skeptical of our ability to specify, a priori, from the ivory tower, how potentially gifted, economically disadvantaged young children will display potential giftedness in their daily lives. Instead, we leave it up to the professionals who see the children daily to use their judgment and tacit knowledge to call to our attention indicators they consider to be important. Thus, we ask the teachers to nominate any children they feel should be looked at more closely and to indicate why the children are being nominated.

Selection of the candidate pool. Once the data described above are gathered, a case-by-case review of each student takes place, involving careful examination of the information in the child's file, considerable discussion, some arguing, and a policy of erring on the side of inclusion. Given the nature of the population, we strive for effectiveness instead of efficiency (Pegnato & Birch, 1959) and aim for a large and inclusive candidate pool of about 35 to 40 students.

Phase II: Diagnostic Assessment

The second phase of identification involves the collection of additional data in individual sessions with each child in the candidate pool (see Figure 2).

Figure 2   Components of Phase II of the Identification Process: Diagnostic
             Assessment

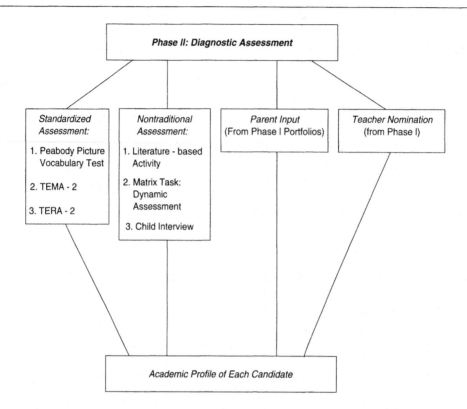

Dynamic assessment: Matrix task. Dynamic assessment, based on Vygotsky's (1978)
"zone of proximal development" and Feuerstein's (1980) "learning potential
assessment," appears to be especially appropriate for this population. The rationale for dynamic assessment is that, instead of measuring what a student
knows and can do at the time of testing, one should gauge what the student is
ready to do or *could* do with a little instruction. Dynamic assessment involves
testing, establishing a level of competency, teaching just beyond that level, and
testing for learning, usually in one sitting.

We designed a matrix task, similar to the items appearing on Raven's
Progressive Matrices (Raven, 1947). In this case, however, each matrix consists
of a 2 x 2 array of attribute blocks that the child can manipulate. The matrix is
presented with the lower right cell empty, and the child has to isolate the relevant row and column characteristics and then combine them to identify the
correct block, from a group placed to the side, to place in the empty cell. Children
who understand the task, apply an effective strategy, and solve many or most
of the items correctly are allowed to complete the test without interruption.
Children who do not solve most of the items correctly are questioned and given
instruction to correct errors in strategy conception or execution. They then
repeat the items missed. This continues until they experience success or it
becomes clear that they are becoming frustrated and success is not forthcoming.

We record the number of correct responses, the number of spontaneous corrections, the number correct following instruction, the child's strategy, and any other behavior displayed. Sessions are videotaped for viewing during the case study described below. Raven (1947) and Spearman (1927) identified tasks of this kind as measures of what the latter called g, and Cattell (1949) believed that matrix activities are good measures of fluid intelligence.

Nontraditional assessment: Literature-based activity. The second author developed a measure based on *The Little Band* (Sage, 1991), a story with minimal text and many ambiguities. First, the story is read to the child. Then questions are posed that (a) require contextual clues and logical reasoning to arrive at a correct answer, (b) require imagination and divergent thinking, (c) test factual knowledge or vocabulary in context, and (d) elicit an affective response. Responses and behaviors are recorded by the team member who works with the child and by another who serves as an observer.

Standardized assessment: Test of Early Mathematics Ability-2. The Test of Early Mathematics Ability-2 (TEMA-2) (Ginsburg & Baroody, 1990) is used to assess early mathematical ability. The TEMA-2 measures formal and informal concepts and skills and, through a series of "probes" or questions, allows one to explore the child's mathematical thinking.

Standardized assessment: Test of Early Reading Ability-2. The Test of Early Reading Ability, 2nd edition (TERA-2) (Reid, Hresko, & Hammill, 1989) is a measure of formal and informal prereading and reading aptitude for young children.

Standardized assessment: Peabody Picture Vocabulary Test. The Peabody Picture Vocabulary Test-Revised (PPVT-R) (Dunn & Dunn, 1981) is a measure of receptive English vocabulary. A test with a strong cultural loading, the PPVT-R might seem to be an odd choice for this population, as would be the case were the scores taken at face value. However, the test does assess an ability important to academic success, and the test's developers recommend it for "screening . . . bright, . . . language-impaired children" (Dunn & Dunn, 1981, p. 3). We interpret the results of this test carefully. Given the language, and experiential deprivation that characterizes the preschool lives of these children, we regard any child who scores near or above the national mean as showing higher-than-average semantic aptitude.

Child interview. Finally, we sit down with each child in the candidate pool for an interview that gives us additional insights into the child's thinking, aspirations, perceptions of parental support, metacognitive awareness, and self-determination (Mithaug, 1991, 1993). Although we are still experimenting with the child interviews, we have found that the children are much more forthcoming than we had expected and that such interviews can be a good source of useful information.

Figure 3   Components of Phase III of the Identification Process: Case Study and Placement Decision

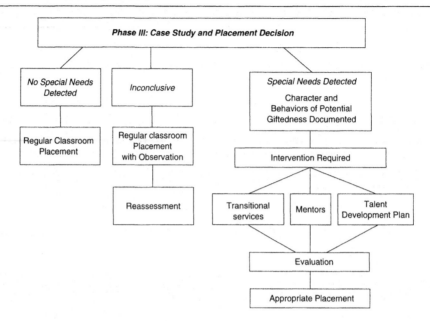

Academic profile of each candidate pool member. The end result of the second phase is a profile of each child in the pool based on the multiple indicators described above, setting the stage for Phase III.

Phase III: Case Study and Placement Decision

Figure 3 shows possible outcomes of Phase III. Each student is placed into a category depending upon whether (a) no signs of potential giftedness are now discernible; (b) equivocal signs are present, requiring further observation and reassessment; or (c) clear signs of potential academic giftedness are present and intervention is indicated. Intervention includes transitional services, mentorships with gifted adolescents (Wright & Borland, 1992), the creation of an individual talent development plan, and parent seminars.

Classifications arc made through a case study process relying on judgment and consensual assessment (Amabile, 1983). The file for each candidate-pool student is carefully examined and discussed in a case conference. Although quantitative data are included in the files, no attempt is made to assign a single composite score to each child. The wealth of information that has been collected over 2 months is too valuable to be lost by placing it on a matrix and attempting to sum nonadditive data. Positive decisions are reached quickly for some children, negative ones for others. For the rest, it is a matter of consideration, debate, and—all else being equal—the need for gender balance, enough Spanish-speaking children, parental support, and other factors.

Once a cohort of students is tentatively identified, we meet with each child's parent or guardian in order to explain the program and to determine whether the parent or guardian is likely to bring the child to transitional services classes (we cover transportation expenses), participate in parent workshops, and, in general, become a more active agent in and advocate for the child's education. Final identification decisions depend on the results of these interviews.

VALIDATION

This process was implemented in the spring of 1991, resulting in the identification of our first cohort, consisting of 18 kindergarten students. On the basis of this experience, we modified the process and used it in academic year 1991–92 to identify our second cohort of 17 children. We made further refinements prior to academic year 1992–93 and identified a third cohort of 17 children. Data bearing on the validity of the process are available for the first two cohorts.

Qualitative Data from the First Cohort

Parents of 14 of the 18 children identified for the first cohort agreed to participate in the project, which began with a 5-week program in the summer of 1991. Of these 14 students, one stopped attending during the first week because of parental indifference and another after 2 weeks because his parents' custody battle frequently made his whereabouts a mystery. Thus there were 12 students who completed the first summer term of transitional-services classes. Because of serious behavior problems, two children, one of whom is now in a class for emotionally disturbed children, were not invited to participate in fall classes (more careful screening for emotional difficulties was instituted in succeeding years).

We thus began 1991–92 with 10 students. During that year, one child moved to another state; one was taken from her crack-addicted mother and disappeared into the foster-care system; and one stopped attending classes despite repeated entreaties to the parents. This left seven children from the first cohort at the end of first grade, six of whom attended nearly every class.

In 1992–93, five students transferred to a school for gifted students, where they have achieved consistently positive teacher evaluations. One of the two students not placed in 1992–93 has been admitted to a parochial school for 1993–94. The other has had social and emotional difficulties, exacerbated by his being taken from his mother by juvenile authorities, and he remains at P.S. 140/207.

That five children were admitted to a selective school for gifted students reflects well on the validity of the process, especially in its first year with no prior field testing. This represents 5% of the 1990–91 kindergarten class of P.S. 149/207, a commonly cited incidence of academic giftedness (Marland, 1972).

Quantitative Data from the First Cohort

First grade data: TEMA-2. The TEMA-2 was administered in July, 1991, in the summer program, and in April, 1992, after a full year of transitional services.

Table 1   Kindergarten and Grade One Test Data for First Cohort: TEMA and TERA

| | TEST OF EARLY MATHEMATICS ABILITY, SECOND EDITION | | | | |
	Date of Testing	n	Mean Math Quotient	Standard Deviation	Median Percentile
Pretest	July, 1991	9	93.7*	12.4	21.0
Posttest	April, 1992	9	105.8*	9.5	69.0

*Difference between means is statistically significant (t (8) = 3.51. p < .01): effect size .097

| | TEST OF EARLY MATHEMATICS ABILITY, SECOND EDITION | | | | |
	Date of Testing	n	Mean Math Quotient	Standard Deviation	Median Percentile
All Ss	April, 1992	10	108.0	10.9	68.5
Active Ss**	April, 1992	6	114.2	7.6	85.5

**Identified students who have participated in all transitional services classes

Increased scores would suggest that the process is valid since we define the target population as potentially gifted students with the capacity to develop academically with intervention. Nine students took both tests, including two who stopped attending transitional-services classes but were still at P.S. 149/207.

The mean pretest mathematics quotient (population mean = 100, SD = 15) was 93.7; the posttest mean was 105.8, a statistically significant difference ($t(8)$ = 3.51, p < .01), with an effect size of 0.97. The pretest median percentile was the 21st, the posttest median percentile the 69th (see Table 1). Thus, these identified students moved as a group from the bottom quarter of the population to the top third, suggesting the kind of potential that characterizes the project's target population.

First grade data: TERA-2. We began using the TERA-2 in 1992; thus, we only have scores reflecting reading ability after a year of transitional services. Ten children at P.S. 149/207 who participated in transitional-services classes to some extent were tested. The mean reading quotient (population mean = 100, SD = 15) was 108.0, the median percentile 68.5. When 4 children who did not participate fully in transitional services were excluded, the mean reading quotient was 114.2, the median percentile 85.5 (see Table 1). Since students received no formal reading instruction before identification, the scores suggest budding academic potential. That this group ranks in the top third nationally after a year of transitional services despite attending a school in which fewer than one child in seven is reading at grade level reflects well on the identification process.

Second grade data: Kaufman Test of Educational Achievement. In late 1992 and early 1993, the five children in the school for gifted students took the Kaufman Test of Educational Achievement (Kaufman & Kaufman, 1985), an individual achievement battery. Although they had spent 2 years in a school where skills were not taught at an appropriate level and 4 months in a school in which teaching mathematics skills was not stressed, scores were encouraging (see Table 2). Battery composites, in percentiles based on national norms, were 99.6, 98.0, 94.0, 47.0. and 5.0, with a median of 94.0. The very low score was obtained by a girl now undergoing educational assessment for a possible learning disability for which she compensated effectively in her previous school, where few academic demands were placed upon her.

Second grade data: Stanford-Binet. In May, 1993, the Stanford-Binet Intelligence Scale: Fourth Edition was administered to the same five children. Since it is known that, in general, economically disadvantaged and minority children score lower on aptitude tests than do middle-class white children, we did not expect Project Synergy children to achieve high scores. Indeed, Project Synergy's *raison d'être* is, in part, to develop alternatives to standardized tests since they are clearly of limited utility in identifying economically disadvantaged gifted children. Nevertheless. although we suspected that the Binet IV would underestimate the children's potential, we wanted, for research purposes, to obtain a conventional measure of general ability for the students who have been in the project for over 2 years and who are now attending a school for gifted students.

The IQs ranged from 104 to 139, with a median of 116 (84th percentile). As a rough comparison, 1991 PPVT IQs for these children ranged from 68 to 109, with a median of 94 (34th percentile). Moreover, there is reason to suspect that the Binet IV depresses scores in the upper range. Silverman and Kearney (1992) describe two studies reported in the test's technical manual of students previously identified as gifted on the basis of the Stanford Binet L-M and the WISC-R. The mean Binet IV scores for these two groups of gifted students were 121.8 and 116.3. Thus, we view the Binet IV scores for this group as encouraging, reflecting gains in general academic aptitude after 2 years of intervention, and we feel they lend additional support to claims that the identification process is valid.

Quantitative Data from the Second Cohort

The second cohort of children was identified in 1991–92, with a concurrent validity check as follows. The director of the Teachers College Child Study Center gave the Jansky Screening Index (Jansky & deHirsh, 1972), a predictor of first grade reading achievement with private school norms, to 60 kindergarten students at P.S. 149/207 while the Project Synergy staff was screening children. Results were not shared with the project staff until our identification was completed. Since placement in more demanding programs is a major project goal, predicted first grade reading achievement relative to independent school expectations was thought to be a useful criterion for assessing the validity of the identification process.

Table 2   Second Grade Test Data for First Cohort

	KAUFMAN TEST OF EDUCATIONAL ACHIEVEMENT Percentile				
	Child 1	Child 2	Child 3	Child 4	Child 5
Reading Decoding	99.0	99.7	98.0	90.0	5.0
Spelling	99.9	99.0	96.0	34.0	12.0
Reading Comprehension	99.0	96.0	87.0	45.0	4.0
Math Computation	98.0	66.0	66.0	13.0	9.0
Math Applications	91.0	37.0	45.0	47.0	37.0
Reading Composite	99.0	99.0	97.0	70.0	4.0
Math Composite	96.0	50.0	55.0	21.0	18.0
Battery Composite	99.6	98.0	94.0	47.0	5.0

	STANFORD-BINET INTELLIGENCE SCALE: FOURTH EDITION Scaled Scores				
	Child 1	Child 2	Child 3	Child 4	Child 5
Verbal Reasoning	136	104	112	126	121
Visual Reasoning	137	130	104	105	103
Quantitative Reasoning	136	112	100	110	96
Short-Term Memory	122	111	102	112	95
Test Composite	139	117	106	116	104

Jansky scores fall into three ranges, (a) scores (=60) indicating a likelihood of solid reading achievement in a private school first grade, (b) borderline scores (53–59) indicating possible at-risk status for first grade reading difficulties, and (c) scores (<52) indicating clear at-risk status for first grade reading difficulties. The mean Jansky score for the 17 students identified by the project as potentially gifted was 62.6, and the mean for 43 unidentified students was 40.6, a statistically significant difference ($t(58) = 6.00$, $p < .001$), with an effect size of 1.7. When unidentified students were separated into students ($n = 26$) who were in the candidate pool and those who were not ($n = 17$), the means were 42.6 and 37.6, a difference that was not statistically significant. Of the identified students, 10 were not at-risk, 3 were borderline, and 4 were at-risk. Of the others, 4 were not at-risk, 3 were borderline, and 30 were at-risk (see Table 3).

Summary of Preliminary Validity Study

These data suggest that the identification process developed as part of Project Synergy has validity for its intended purpose, the identification of young economically disadvantaged children with the potential for academic giftedness. More conclusive evidence must await longitudinal study of identified students in their new placements, now in progress (Borland et al., in preparation).

Table 3   Kindergarten Jansky Screening Index Results for the Second Cohort

JANSKY MEANS AND STANDARD DEVIATIONS FOR THREE GROUPS

Group	N	Mean	SD
Identified	17	62.8	14.2
Pool but not Identified	26	42.6	12.3
Not in Pool: Not Identified	17	37.6	12.2

*The difference between identified group and other two groups was statistically significant; $t(58) = 6.00$, $p < .001$.

CROSS-TABULATION OF AT-RISK STATUS BY IDENTIFICATION STATUS

At-Risk Status	Not in Pool	Identification Status Pool, Not Identified	Identified
At-Risk	16	20	4
Possibly At-Risk	0	3	3
Not At Risk	1	3	10

CONCLUSION

The procedures described here are admittedly time- and labor-intensive. One could legitimately question the practicability of their implementation in a typical school setting. Clearly, our research, and that of others, must move us in the direction of valid methods that are more economical of time and energy. However, at this stage in the development of our field, that is not the major issue.

As we discuss above, our field has not succeeded as we all would like with respect to the issue of equity. Failure stems from a lack of methods but also, we suspect, from an underlying uncertainty as to whether this kind of education really has meaning in schools beset by the problems found in many urban schools. Our work at P.S. 149/207 demonstrates that even in the most beleaguered schools there are children with the potential for academic giftedness, academic giftedness without quotation marks or qualifiers.

Refining and streamlining our methods, and those developed by others, is necessary, but the motivation needs to come from a belief that giftedness can be found in every school, if one only looks. Should this belief become widespread in education, we will have no excuse, methodological or otherwise, for not succeeding where, in the past, despite our best intentions, we have failed.

REFERENCES

Amabile, T. M. (1983). *The social psychology of creativity.* New York: Springer.

Borland, J. H. (1989). *Planning and implementing programs for the gifted.* Education and Psychology of the Gifted Series. New York: Teachers College Press.

Borland, J. H., Horowitz, J., Kearney, K., Kogan-Frenk, E., McMahon, J., Schnur, R., Simons, J., Wilcove, J., & Wright, L. (in preparation). Economically disadvantaged students in a school for the academically gifted: A postpositivist inquiry into individual and family adjustment.

Cattell, R. B. (1949). *The culture free intelligence test.* Champaign, IL: Institute for Personality Research and Testing.

Chittenden, E. (1991). Authentic assessment, evaluation, and documentation of student performance. In V. Perrone (Ed.). *Expanding student assessment* (pp. 22–31). Alexandria, VA: Association for Supervision and Curriculum Development.

Dunn, L. M., & Dunn, L. M. (1981). *Peabody picture vocabulary test-revised.* Circle Pines, MN: American Guidance Service.

Feuerstein, R. (1980). *Instrumental enrichment: An intervention program for cognitive modifiability.* Baltimore, MD: University Park Press.

Gallagher, J. J. (1985). *Teaching the gifted child* (3rd ed.). Newton, MA: Allyn and Bacon.

Ginsburg, H. P., & Baroody, A. (1990). *Test of early mathematics ability* (2nd ed.). Austin, TX: PRO-ED.

Harris, D. (1963). *Children's drawings as measures of intellectual maturity: A revision and extension of the Goodenough draw-a-man test.* New York: Harcourt Brace & World.

Howley, A., Howley, C. B., & Pendarvis, E. D. (1986). *Teaching gifted children: Principles and strategies.* Boston: Little, Brown and Company.

Jansky, J. J., & deHirsh, K. (1972). The screening index. In J. J. Jansky & K. deHirsh (Eds.). *Preventing reading failures* (pp. 77–108). New York: Harper & Row.

Jensen, A. R. (1980). *Bias in mental testing.* New York: The Free Press.

Kaufman, A. S., & Kaufman, N. L. (1985). *Kaufman test of educational achievement.* Circle Pines, MN: American Guidance Service.

Kozol, J. (1991). *Savage inequalities.* New York: Crown.

Lincoln, Y. S., & Guba, E. G. (1985). *Naturalistic inquiry.* Beverly Hills, CA: Sage.

Marland, S. J. (1972). *Education of the gifted and talented. Report to Congress.* Washington, DC: U.S. Government Printing Office.

Myers, D. G. (1991, January 16). Don't all children have gifts? *Education Week,* p. 36.

Mithaug, D. E. (1991). *Self-determined kids. Raising satisfied and successful children.* Lexington, MA: Lexington Books.

Mithaug, D. E. (1993). *Self-regulation theory: How optimal adjustment maximizes gain.* Westport. CT: Praeger.

Natriello, G., McDill, E. L., & Pallas, A. M. (1990). *Schooling disadvantaged children: Racing against catastrophe.* New York: Teachers College Press.

Ogbu, J. U. (1985). *Minority education and caste: The American system in cross cultural perspective.* New York: Academic Press.

Ogbu, J. U. (1992). Understanding cultural diversity and learning. *Educational Researcher, 21*(8), 5–14.

Passow, A. H. (1989). Needed research and development in educating high ability children. *Roeper Review, 11,* 223–229.

Pegnato, C. W., & Birch, J. W. (1959). Locating gifted children in junior high school. *Exceptional Children, 25,* 300–304.

Raven, J. (1947). *Raven's progressive matrices test.* London: H. K. Lewis.

Reid, D. K., Hresko, W. P., & Hammill, D. D. (1989). *Test of early reading ability* (2nd ed.). Rockville, MD: PRO-ED.

Richert, E. S. (1987). Rampant problems and promising practices in the identification of disadvantaged gifted students. *Gifted Child Quarterly, 31,* 149–154.

Roedell, W. C., Jackson, N. E., & Robinson, H. B. (1980). *Gifted young children.* Perspectives on Gifted and Talented Education. New York: Teachers College Press.

Sage, J. (1991). *The little band.* New York: Macmillan.

Silverman, L. K., & Kearney, K. (1992). The case for the Stanford-Binet L-M as a supplemental test. *Roeper Review, 15,* 34–37.

Slavin, R. E. (1991). Are cooperative learning and "untracking" harmful to the gifted? Response to Allan. *Educational Leadership, 49*(3), 68–71.

Spearman, C. (1927). *The abilities of man.* London: Macmillan.

Tannenbaum, A. J. (1983). *Gifted children: Psychological and educational perspectives.* New York: Macmillan.

United States Department of Education. (1991). *National educational longitudinal study 88. Final report: Gifted and talented education programs for eighth-grade public school students.* Washington DC: United States Department of Education. Office of Planning, Budget, and Evaluation.

Van Tassel-Baska, J., Patton, J., & Prillaman, D. (1989). Disadvantaged gifted learners: At risk for educational attention. *Focus on Exceptional Children, 22*(3) 1–15.

Vygotsky, L. (1978). *Mind in society.* Cambridge, MA: Harvard University Press.

Wright, L., & Borland, J. H. (1992). A special friend: Adolescent mentors for young, economically disadvantaged, potentially gifted students. *Roeper Review, 14,* 124–129.

Wright, L., & Borland, J. H. (1993). Using portfolios in the identification of young, economically disadvantaged, potentially gifted students. *Roeper Review, 15,* 205–210.

5

Nonentrenchment in the Assessment of Intellectual Giftedness

Robert J. Sternberg

It is customary in the literature on giftedness to distinguish between intelligence, on the one hand, and creativity, on the other (e.g., Renzulli, 1980). This theoretical distinction is reinforced by, and to some extent is responsible for, differences in the prototypical contents of tests purporting to measure intelligence or creativity. Intelligence tests typically require students to demonstrate large vocabularies, high reading comprehension, rapid and accurate spatial visualization, facility in solving mathematical problems, and the like; creativity tests typically require students to generate unusual uses for products, to think of unusual questions, to take givens in pictures and incorporate them into more complex pictures, etc. Using Guilford's (1967) terminology, one might characterize the intelligence tests as tending more to require "convergent" thinking to a single best answer, and the creativity tests as tending more to require "divergent" thinking to multiple answers, some of which are better in some sense

Editor's Note: From Sternberg, R. J. (1982). Nonentrenchment in the assessment of intellectual giftedness. *Gifted Child Quarterly*, 26(2), 88-94. © 1982 National Association for Gifted Children. Reprinted with permission.

(e.g., more novel) than others, but no one of which is uniquely correct. It is interesting that Guilford's terms so well characterize the difference between the two kinds of tests, because Guilford has been one of a small number of theorists who has integrated the theory and measurement of creativity and intelligence under the umbrella of a single model of intellect.

The distinction between convergent and divergent thinking is not the only one that separates the measurement of creativity from the measurement of intelligence. My contention in this article is that there exists at least one other source of separation that is unfortunate if one's goal is to measure the kind of creative or flexible intelligence that many of us concerned with the gifted may most want to assess. This distinction may serve to highlight the differences between intelligence and creativity at the same time that it serves to obscure similarities between them. My proposal is that there is a confounding between "entrenchment" and "nonentrenchment," and between the measurement of intelligence and of creativity. In order to explicate the nature of this confounding, and to propose a remedy for it, I must first define my terms.

THE NATURE OF NONENTRENCHMENT

"Entrenchment" and "nonentrenchment" are terms drawn from the philosophy of induction (Goodman, 1955, 1972), but which I believe are relevant as well in the understanding and measurement of human abilities (Sternberg, 1981c). By "entrenchment," I refer to naturalness in the run of everyday experience. Something that is well entrenched is a natural part of a person's everyday experience; something that is nonentrenched is unnatural, or strange, with respect to a person's everyday experience. Note that entrenchment is not the same as mere familiarity. For example, turnips and collard greens are by no means part of my everyday experience (and purposely so!), but neither are they unnatural in my experience. Hence, they are relatively unfamiliar to me, but nevertheless entrenched. Entrenchment and nonentrenchment can apply to a variety of objects, but for the purpose of understanding human abilities and their measurement, I believe two objects are especially relevant: tasks and concepts.

Consider first the level of tasks. An entrenched task is one that is natural in everyday experience. For students, tasks such as reading a passage for comprehension or solving mathematical problems are entrenched tasks. A nonentrenched task is one that is unnatural in everyday experience. Generating unusual uses for products or incorporating simple drawings (lines, half circles, and the like) into more complex original drawings are nonentrenched tasks for students.

Consider next the level of concepts. An entrenched concept is one that is natural in everyday experience—people feel comfortable with it. For example, "planet" is a fairly well entrenched concept: Students know what planets are, what some of their properties are (e.g., that they are usually solid, that they revolve around a star, that they often have moons, etc.), and how they are identified (e.g., via the naked eye or a telescope). A nonentrenched concept is one that is unnatural or strange in everyday experience. For example, "black hole" is a relatively nonentrenched concept: It is hard to conceive of objects in which gravity is so strong that light cannot escape, in which time comes to a standstill at their center, and which are dense to a point that virtually defies imagination. For students, the concepts encountered in typical reading passages or mathematical problems are fairly well entrenched; the concept of a world in which there is a great fog such that only people's feet can be seen is relatively nonentrenched (Torrance, 1966).

If one examines the content of intelligence tests, as well as creativity tests, one is likely to arrive at a fairly simple generalization: Intelligence tests tend to include both tasks and concepts that are for the most part entrenched; creativity tests tend to include tasks that are for the most part nonentrenched, and they often include nonentrenched concepts as well. Some of the examples noted above are applicable to the differentiation, and numerous other examples could be cited as well. Subtests found on intelligence tests such as synonyms, reading comprehension, solving mathematical problems, solving analogies, and completing number series are relatively entrenched in our culture. In the case of some of these subtests, such as analogies and number series, it may be the very existence of the tests that has made the tasks entrenched. But whatever the origin of the set of experiences may be, by the time a student is in high school, the student has been subjected to a barrage of standardized tests and teacher-made exercises that require skills similar or identical to those required in the solution of intelligence-test problems. Not all tasks on intelligence tests are highly entrenched: For example, three-dimensional paper folding would seem to be less entrenched than is reading comprehension. But for the most part, the tasks are relatively highly entrenched. Subtests found on creativity tests such as product improvement, unusual uses, and picture completion (Torrance, 1966) involve tasks that are relatively nonentrenched in the student culture. Students taking creativity tests often encounter tasks and concepts that are rather different in kind from any they have encountered in the past and that may, indeed, seem quite strange and unnatural, independent of their level of difficulty.

It is possible to increase the difficulty of a class of tasks by using relatively more nonentrenched variants of the tasks or the concepts they employ. This variation in nonentrenchment would be quite normal in a graded series of creativity tasks. For example, it might be more difficult to think of unusual uses of two overlapping poles attached by a C-clamp than it would be to think of unusual uses for the common paper clip. But variations in nonentrenchment are rarely sources of increased difficulty in intelligence tests. Vocabulary is usually increased in difficulty by the use of less familiar words, but not by the use of concepts underlying words that are relatively more strange or unnatural. More difficult mathematics problems may require more sophisticated or less familiar mathematical knowledge and know-how, but except for occasional "insight" problems, the harder problems are no less natural than the easier ones. Even in analogies, where one might expect increased difficulty to result from increasing bizarreness of relations, one usually finds that increases in difficulty are due primarily to increased difficulty of vocabulary (see Sternberg, 1981b).

In general, then, entrenchment and nonentrenchment are pretty well confounded with the measurement of intelligence and creativity, just as are convergent and divergent thinking. But I contend that whereas the latter distinction is appropriate because it is inherent in the respective natures of intelligence which tends primarily to be convergent, and creativity, which tends primarily to be divergent, the latter distinction is most unfortunate and is inappropriate if we wish to measure the kinds of creative and flexible intelligence that are truly important in consequential problem solving.

INTELLIGENCE AND NONENTRENCHMENT

Intelligence comprises, in large part, the ability to acquire and think in terms of novel kinds of concepts and conceptual systems. It is not so much a person's ability to learn or think within conceptual systems that the person has already become familiar with as it is his or her ability to assimilate systems that at first seem strange, and then to bring already existing knowledge structures and skills to bear on these new systems. On this view, valid measurements of intelligence should require more of the flexible and novel kinds of thinking that are currently measured by creativity tests, while at the same time maintaining the emphasis upon analytic skills that has characterized intelligence tests and distinguished them from creativity tests. Stated otherwise, I find the distinction between the convergent tasks that have typified the measurement of intelligence and the divergent tasks that have typified the measurement of creativity to be a useful one: Analytic intelligence and synthetic creativity are, I believe, distinguishable abilities, and there is much to be gained by attempting as best we can to measure them differentially. A person who is good at solving problems is not necessarily good at finding them; from the complementary perspective, a person who is good at generating ideas is not necessarily good at analyzing the implications of these (or other) ideas. But whereas the convergent-divergent distinction may be useful in distinguishing intelligence from creativity, I do not believe the entrenched-nonentrenched one is.

This view seems consistent with many of our everyday notions about intelligence, if not always with our research about or measurement of it. A student is likely to be considered more intelligent if he or she can master a new kind of course (say, calculus or foreign language) than if he or she can master another course that differs in substance but not in kind from courses the student has taken previously. We tend to be less impressed with students (or scientists, for that matter) who merely demonstrate time and again the competence they have already demonstrated many times before than we are with students (or scientists) who are continually demonstrating new kinds of competencies. Indeed, the most successful students and scientists are often those who bring new conceptual systems to bear on old problems. The ability to do so is certainly a distinguishing mark of giftedness.

One might speculate that the view presented here was one of the implicit philosophical underpinnings that motivated the notion of a "classical education." Students exposed to Latin or Greek were exposed not only to another language, but to a language that in many respects differed in kind from the English (or other) language they had learned to speak as young children. Similarly, students exposed to the ideas of great classical scholars such as Plato or Aristotle were confronted with ways of thinking that probably differed from any they had previously been accustomed to. Almost anyone confronted for the first time with a Platonic dialogue or seeking to understand Plato's concept of idealism will have to stretch her or his thinking in new ways never before experienced. In contrast, exposure only to ideas from the culture to which one belongs is less likely to confront the student with nonentrenched concepts, precisely because the culture defines what becomes entrenched for its members: What is natural for members of one culture may be bizarre and unnatural for members of another culture, as anthropologists have discovered time and again.

To summarize, then, intelligence seems to consist in large part of the ability to deal with nonentrenched tasks and concepts, but this ability seems only to be peripherally measured by current tests of intelligence. Failing to measure this ability may trivialize, at least in some degree, our measurements of intelligence, especially at the upper levels, where novel ways of thinking may be critical to success. The great minds of the century—Chomsky, Einstein, Piaget, Skinner, to name a few—are considered great in part because their contributions were so nonentrenched. They saw old things in new ways that provided insights that had previously escaped their peers.

NONENTRENCHMENT IN MEASUREMENT

In order to illustrate how the notions presented above can be applied to measurements of intelligence, I will draw at length upon a domain with which I am quite familiar—analogies. I will then discuss more briefly how these notions might be applied to other kinds of problems as well.

A typical analogies task requires an examinee to choose the correct completion to an item taking a form such as A: B :: C : (D_1, D_2, D_3, D_4), where the first three terms are givens and the last four (or whatever number) are multiple-choice response alternatives. Items are usually made more difficult by increasing the complexity of the terms—for example, more difficult vocabulary in verbal analogies or more complicated geometric figures in figural analogies—or by increasing the complexity of the relations characterizing the terms of the analogy, for example, A to B, A to C, and so on (see Sternberg, 1977, for details on a theory describing these relations). If the relations are made more novel as well as merely more obscure in the difficult items, then these items may be more difficult by virtue of increased nonentrenchment as well as by virtue of sheer unfamiliarity. In my experience, however, obscurity tends to play a larger role in analogy difficulty than does nonentrenchment. But there are ways of making analogies more difficult that do capitalize upon the potential inherent in analogies for manipulating nonentrenchment. What are some of these ways?

1. *Nonentrenchment of concepts.* It is possible to use nonentrenched concepts in the terms of the analogies. For example, Rumelhart and Abrahamson (1973) gave subjects a concept-learning task in which the subjects had to learn the meanings of new "mammal" concepts by solving analogies containing them, for example, SHEEP : CAT :: BOF : (a) RABBIT, (b) CHIMPANZEE, (c) LEOPARD, (d) BEAR. Using this paradigm, one can measure students' ability to solve the analogies both while they are learning the meanings of the newly created mammals (in Rumelhart and Abrahamson's case, BOF, DAX, and ZUK), and once they have already learned them. Whitely and Barnes (1979) had subjects solve analogies based on supposed life forms that could evolve on other planets. Subjects would receive an analogy such as LYOMON : FIRMANI :: DUCIVER : (a) BANSHER, (b) PONTO, (c) NAX, (d) SQUISH, and would have the opportunity explicitly to request information about each animal. For example, the subject could request information that would inform him or her that a squish (a) lives on a high gravity world, (b) does not migrate, (c) is an aquatic predator, (d) swims by jet propulsion with gills and a tail, and (e) is evolutionarily an old animal. The authors also had pictures of the supposed animals. It is possible to create analogies with relatively nonentrenched concepts that are less exotic than are the analogies above. For example, an analogy such as I : V :: X : (a) C, (b) L, (c) D, (d) Z, is difficult because solution of the analogy requires the examinee to disregard the relatively more entrenched meanings of each of the terms—letters of the alphabet—in favor of relatively less entrenched meanings of the terms—Roman numerals. The terms are familiar and the relations between them simple. What is complicated is the recognition of the relatively less entrenched use of the analogy terms. Similarly, the analogy, STEP : PETS :: REEL : (a) FISHES, (b) ROD, (c) LEER, (d) REAL, is made difficult by the relatively nonentrenched use of sets of letters and letters placed in reverse order in the analogy. One tends to see the more entrenched use of the symbols—words—before seeing the less entrenched use of the symbols—letter strings devoid of semantic implications.

2. *Nonentrenchment of relations.* It is possible to use entrenched concepts in the terms of the analogies but to draw upon nonentrenched relations between them. Several investigators, for example, have used analogies based upon mammal names to study analogical reasoning skills (Rumelhart & Abrahamson, 1973; Sternberg, 1977; Sternberg & Gardner, in press). An example of such an analogy would be CAT : LION :: DOG : (a) FOX, (b) ELEPHANT, (c) WOLF, (d) GORILLA. Subjects were found to draw upon relations between animals in size, ferocity, and humanness in solving these analogies. The terms of the analogies are quite entrenched, but the idea of solving analogies with mammal terms is quite nonentrenched. Again, it is possible to construct nonentrenched analogies that are less exotic. The analogy, WASHINGTON : 1 :: LINCOLN : (a) 2, (b) 5, (c) 10, (d) 15, is fairly difficult because it often takes some time to recognize that

the relation is one of the kind of currency on which the portrait of the relevant president appears. Much more entrenched, perhaps, is the relation of ordinal order of presidency, which happens to be irrelevant in the present instance. Similarly, IMPEACH : 1 :: CONVICT : (a) 0, (b) 2, (c) 3, (d) 5, may be difficult primarily because it takes some time to recognize that the relation is one of the number of presidents of the United States who have been successfully subjected to the given proceeding.

3. *Nonentrenchment of task variant.* It is possible to use entrenched concepts and relations in an analogy, but to present the concepts and relations in a nonentrenched way. A minor manipulation of task nonentrenchment can be attained by having the missing term be one other than the last one, as is done in the Miller Analogies Test. A slightly more significant manipulation has two analogy terms missing. For example, the Scholastic Aptitude Test requires subjects to decide on what the last two terms ought to be, and the Differential Aptitude Test has subjects decide what the first and last terms should be. But all items within the given test have the same format. Bill Salter and I attained a more substantial manipulation by having as missing terms either one, two, or three items, with the particular identities of the items varying over items. For example, there were items of the forms $(A_1, A_2, A_3) : B :: C (D_1, D_2, D_3)$, $A : (B_1, B_2, B_3) :: (C_1, C_2, C_3) : D$, $(A_1, A_2, A_3) : (B_1, B_2, B_3) :: (C_1, C_2, C_3) : D$, and of seven other forms as well. In one condition of presentation, items were thoroughly mixed so that all formats appeared on a given test. A concrete example of such an item would be MAN : (SKIN, PETS) :: (DOG, TREE) : BARK. Our particular paradigm had the advantage of actually enabling us to separate out a "nonentrenchment" parameter for each individual subject. This parameter was, in fact, significantly correlated with scores from standardized mental tests for the college-level sample we used in our study (see Sternberg, 1981c). Still other nonentrenched formats are possible: For example Cathryn Downing and I presented adolescent subjects with higher-order analogies, that is, analogies between analogies, such as BENCH : JUDGE :: PULPIT : MINISTER :: HAIR : HEAD :: GRASS : LAWN, and asked the subjects to rate the goodness of the higher-order analogy between analogies. We devised a measure of goodness of performance on the test, and found it, too, was significantly correlated with intellectual ability level (Sternberg & Downing, 1982).

I have dwelled at some length on the manipulation of nonentrenchment through analogy tasks because analogies have been a central task in both theorizing (Spearman, 1923; Sternberg, 1977) and measurement of intelligence, and because I am relatively familiar with the task from my own research. But another way to go in the measurement of ability to handle nonentrenched tasks and concepts is to devise new kinds of measurements entirely. For example, I have devised a task loosely based upon Goodman's (1955) "new riddle of induction." I will give only a casual description of the task and resulting data here. Much more detail is contained in Sternberg (1981c, 1981d).

Subjects were presented with a description of the color of an object in the present day and in the year 2000. The description could be either physical—a green dot or a blue dot—or verbal—one of our color words, namely, *green, blue, grue,* or *bleen.* An object was defined as green if it appeared physically green both in the present and in the year 2000. An object was defined as blue if it appeared physically blue both in the present and in the year 2000. An object was defined as grue if it appeared physically green in the present but physically blue in the year 2000 (i.e., it appeared physically green until the year 2000 and physically blue thereafter). An object was defined as bleen if it appeared physically blue in the present but physically green in the year 2000 (i.e., it appeared physically blue until the year 2000 and physically green thereafter).

Since each of the two descriptions (one in the present and one in the year 2000) could take one of either two physical forms or four verbal forms, there were 36 (6×6) different item types. The subject's task was to describe the object in the year 2000. If the given description for the year 2000 was a physical one, the subject had to indicate the correct verbal description of the object; if the given description for the year 2000 was a verbal one, the subject had to indicate the correct physical description of the object. There were always three answer choices from which the subject had to choose the correct one. Certain complexities were introduced by the fact that verbal descriptions in the present were not always reliable, but these complexities will not be described here. Consider, though, a typical item: GREEN, (B) : (a) GRUE, (b) BLEEN, (c) GREEN, where GREEN is a verbal description of the object in the present, (B) represents a blue dot showing the physical appearance of the object in the year 2000, and GRUE, BLEEN, and GREEN are answer options. The correct answer is (a), since the object transited from green to blue physical appearance at the year 2000. Subjects' latencies on this task and on other variants of it were rather highly correlated with psychometrically measured intellectual ability (with correlations in the range from .4 to .8). The fact that the correlations were rather high but not perfect is consistent with the notion that these tests tap something similar but nonidentical to what is tapped by standard intelligence tests. They tap an ability to handle a nonentrenched task containing nonentrenched concepts— something that most IQ tests simply do not measure, or at least, measure well.

CONCLUSION

I have argued in this article for an expanded notion of intelligence, in general, and of intellectual giftedness, in particular, that takes heed of a person's ability to learn and reason with nonentrenched tasks and concepts. This view brings the concept of intelligence closer to that of creativity, as usually conceived, but still maintains the distinction between convergent and divergent thinking that has traditionally characterized the difference between what is measured in intelligence tests and what is measured in creativity tests. It is claimed that the distinction between convergent and divergent thinking is orthogonal to that between working with entrenched and nonentrenched tasks and concepts. In existing tests, however, these two distinctions are confounded, so that measurement of convergent and entrenched thinking tend to go together, and measurement of divergent and nonentrenched thinking tend to go together. This should not be the case, and I have given examples of how it need not be. Although the measurement of the ability to deal with nonentrenched tasks and concepts is not sufficient for the assessment of intellectual giftedness, I believe it is necessary (see Sternberg, 1981a, for presentation of a more wide-ranging account of intellectual giftedness). When we measure performance on nonentrenched tasks or with nonentrenched concepts, I believe we will then be measuring one very important ability that distinguishes the intellectually gifted from the rest of the population.

REFERENCES

Goodman, N. *Fact, fiction, and forecast.* Cambridge, MA: Harvard University Press, 1955.

Goodman, N. *Problems and projects.* Indianapolis: Bobbs-Merrill, 1972.

Guilford, J. P. *The nature of human intelligence.* NYC: McGraw-Hill, 1967.

Renzulli, J. S. Will the gifted child movement be alive and well in 1990? *Gifted Child Quarterly,* 1980, 24, 3–9.

Rumelhart, D. E., & Abrahamson, A. A. A model for analogical reasoning. *Cognitive Psychology,* 1973, 5, 1–28.

Spearman, C. *The nature of 'intelligence' and the principles of cognition.* London: Macmillan, 1923.

Sternberg, R J. *Intelligence, information processing, and analogical reasoning*: The componential analysis of human abilities. Hillsdale, NJ: Erlbaum, 1977.

Sternberg, R. J. A componential theory of intellectual giftedness. *Gifted Child Quarterly,* 1981, 25, 86–93. (a)

Sternberg, R. J. *How to prepare for the Miller analogies test* (3rd ed.). Woodbury, NY: Barron's Educational Series, 1981. (b)

Sternberg, R. J. Intelligence and nonentrenchment. *Journal of Educational Psychology,* 1981, 73, 1–16. (c)

Sternberg, R. J. *Natural, unnatural, and supernatural concepts.* Manuscript submitted for publication, 1981. (d)

Sternberg, R. J., & Downing, C. J. The development of higher-order reasoning in adolescence. *Child Development,* 1982, 53, 209–221.

Sternberg, R. J., & Gardner, M. K. A componential interpretation of the general factor in human intelligence. In H. J. Eysenck (Ed.), *A model for intelligence.* Heidelberg: Springer-Verlag, in press.

Torrance, E. P. *The Torrance tests of creative thinking.* Lexington, MA: Ginn, 1966.

Whitely, S. E., & Barnes, G. M. The implications of processing event sequences for theories of analogical reasoning. *Memory and Cognition,* 1979, 7, 323–331.

6

Lies We Live By: Misapplication of Tests in Identifying the Gifted

Robert J. Sternberg

In the large majority of school systems, standardized tests play a major part in screening programs for identifying the gifted. By and large, tests can play and probably do play a valuable role in assessment, identifying students of exceptional talent and screening out students of lesser gifts. The better intelligence tests, at least, have shown sufficient validity and reliability for screening purposes when they are used in conjunction with other criteria.

My contention in this article, however, is that tests only work for some of the people some of the time—not for all of the people all of the time—and that certain assumptions we make in our use of tests are, at best, correct only for a segment of the tested population, and at worst, correct for none of it. As a result, we fail to identify many gifted individuals for whom the assumptions underlying our use of tests are particularly inadequate. The problem, then, is not only that tests are of limited validity for everyone, but that their validity varies

Editor's Note: From Sternberg, R. J. (1982). Lies we live by: Misapplication of tests in identifying the gifted. *Gifted Child Quarterly, 26*(4), 157-161. © 1982 National Association for Gifted Children. Reprinted with permission.

across individuals: For some people, test scores may be quite informative; for others, such scores may be worse than useless. Use of test-score cutoffs and formulas results in a serious problem of underidentification of gifted children.

What dubious assumptions underlie our use of standardized tests? There are undoubtedly many, but I would like to dwell on four assumptions here. Blind, across-the-board acceptance of these assumptions, I would maintain, is widespread, but wrong.

Dubious Assumption #1: To be smart is to be fast. The assumption that "smart is fast" permeates our entire society. When we refer to someone as "quick," we are endowing them with one of the primary attributes of what we perceive an intelligent person to be. Indeed, in a recent study of people's conceptions of intelligence, when we asked people to list behaviors characteristic of intelligent persons, behaviors such as "learns rapidly," "acts quickly," "talks quickly," and "makes judgments quickly" were commonly listed (Sternberg, Conway, Ketron, & Bernstein, 1981). It is not only the man in the street who believes that speed is associated with intellect. Several prominent contemporary theorists of intelligence base their theories in large part upon individual differences in the speed with which people process information (e.g., Hunt, 1978; Jensen, 1979).

The assumption that more intelligent people are rapid information processors also underlies the overwhelming majority of tests used in identification of the gifted, including creativity as well as intelligence tests. It is rare to find a test that is not timed, or a timed test that virtually all examinees are able to finish by working at a comfortable rate of problem solving. I would argue that this assumption is a gross overgeneralization: It is true for some people and for some mental operations, but not for all people or all mental operations. Blind, across-the-board acceptance of the assumption is not only unjustified—it is wrong.

Almost everyone knows people who, although often slow in performing tasks, perform the tasks at a superior level of accomplishment. Moreover, we all know that snap judgments are often poor ones. Indeed, in our study of people's conceptions of intelligence, "does not make snap judgments" was listed as an important attribute of intelligent performance. Evidence for the dubiousness of the "smart is fast" assumption extends, however, beyond intuition and everyday observation. A number of findings from carefully conducted psychological research undermine the validity of the assumption. I will cite four such findings, which are only examples from a wider literature on the subject.

First, it is well known that, in general, a *reflective* rather than an *impulsive* style in problem solving tends to be associated with more intelligent problem-solving performance (see Baron, 1981, 1982, for reviews of this literature). Jumping into problems without adequate reflection is likely to lead to false starts and erroneous conclusions. Yet, timed tests often force the examinee to solve problems impulsively. It is often claimed that the strict timing of such tests merely mirrors the requirements of our highly pressured and productive society. But ask yourself how many significant problems you encounter in your work or personal life that allow no more than the 15 to 60 seconds allowed for a typical test problem on a standardized test; you will probably be hard pressed to think of any such problems.

Second, in a study of the role of planning behavior in problem solving, it has been found that more intelligent persons tend to spend relatively more time than do less intelligent persons on global (higher-order, up-front) planning, and relatively less time on local (problem-specific, lower-level) planning. In contrast, less intelligent persons show the reverse pattern, emphasizing local rather than global planning (relative to the more intelligent persons) (Sternberg, 1981). The point is that what matters is not total time spent, but distribution of this time across the various kinds of planning one can do.

Third, in studies of reasoning behavior in children and adults, it has been found that although greater intelligence is associated with more rapid execution of most components of information processing, problem encoding is a notable exception to this trend. The more intelligent individuals tend to spend relatively more time encoding the terms of the problem, presumably in order to facilitate subsequent operations on these encodings (see Mulholland, Pellegrino, & Glaser, 1980; Sternberg, 1977; Sternberg & Rifkin, 1979). Similar outcomes have been observed in comparisons of expert versus novice problem solvers confronted with difficult physics problems (Chi, Glaser, & Rees, 1982).

Finally, in a study of people's performance in solving insight problems (arithmetical and logical problems whose difficulty resided in the need for a nonobvious insight for problem solution rather than in the need of arithmetical or logical knowledge), a correlation of .75 was found between the amount of time people spent on the problems and measured IQ. The correlation between time spent and score on the insight problems was .62 (Sternberg & Davidson, 1982). Note that in these problems individuals were free to spend as long as they liked solving the problems. Persistence and involvement in the problems was highly correlated with success in solution. The more able individuals did not give up, nor did they fall for the obvious, but often incorrect, solutions.

The point of these examples is simple: Sometimes speed is desirable; sometimes it is not. Whether it is desirable or not depends upon the task, the particular component of information processing involved in solution of the task, and, most likely, the person's style of problem solving. Blind imposition of a strict time limit for a test, or even a not-so-strict one, is theoretically indefensible, and practically self-defeating.

Dubious Assumption #2: Intelligence is last year's achievement. At first glance, this would appear to be an assumption few people would accept. Indeed, doesn't almost everyone make a clear distinction between intelligence and achievement? But if one examines the content of the major intelligence tests currently in use, one will find that most of them measure intelligence as last year's (or the year before's or the year before that's) achievement. What is an intelligence test for children of a given age would be an achievement test for children a few years younger. In some test items, like vocabulary, the achievement component is obvious. In others, it is more disguised, for example, verbal analogies or arithmetic problems. But virtually all tests commonly used for the assessment of intelligence place heavy achievement demands on the students tested.

The achievement-testing orientation exhibited in intelligence tests may be acceptable and even appropriate when the tests are administered to children who have had fully adequate educational opportunities in reasonably adequate social and emotional environments. But for children whose environments have been characterized by deprivation of one kind or another, the orientation may lead to invalid test results. There is no fully adequate solution to the problem of identification of the gifted among such youngsters, especially if the youngsters will have to function in the normal socio-cultural milieu. A common solution to the problem—exclusive use of nonverbal tests—is almost certainly an inadequate solution: First, one is measuring only a subset of important intellectual skills; second, and perhaps more importantly, nonverbal tests actually show, on the average, greater differences in scores across socio-cultural groups than do verbal ones (Jensen, 1980; Lesser, Fifer, & Clark, 1965). An alternative solution to the problem is to ask what abilities one is really interested in measuring by the achievement-saturated tests, and then to attempt to measure these abilities more directly and in ways that reduce the achievement load. This is the path we have followed. Here are two examples.

Consider first one of the most common types of items on intelligence tests—vocabulary. It is well known that vocabulary is one of the best predictors, if not the best single predictor, of overall IQ score (Jensen, 1980; Matarazzo, 1972). Yet, few tests have higher achievement load than does vocabulary. Can one measure the latent ability tapped by vocabulary tests without presenting children with what is essentially an achievement test? I believe one can.

There is reason to believe that vocabulary is such a good measure of intelligence because it measures, albeit indirectly, children's ability to acquire information in context (Jensen, 1980; Sternberg, Powell, & Kaye, 1982; Werner & Kaplan, 1952). Most vocabulary is learned in everyday contexts rather than through direct instruction. Thus, new words are usually encountered for the first time (and subsequently) in textbooks, novels, newspapers, lectures, and the like. More intelligent people are better able to use surrounding context to figure out the words' meanings. As the years go by, the better decontextualizers acquire the larger vocabularies. Because so much of one's learning (including learning beside vocabulary) is contextually determined, the ability to use context to add to one's knowledge base is an important skill in intelligent behavior. Is there any way of measuring this skill directly, rather than relying on indirect measurement (vocabulary testing) that involves a heavy achievement load? We have attempted to measure this skill directly by presenting children with paragraphs written at a level well below their grade level. Embedded in the paragraphs are one or more unknown words. The children's task is to use the surrounding context to figure out the meanings of the unknown words. Note that in this testing paradigm, differential effects of past achievement are reduced by using reading passages that are easy for everyone, but target vocabulary words that are unknown to everyone. We have found that quality of children's definitions of the unknown words is highly correlated with overall verbal intelligence, reading comprehension, and vocabulary test scores (about .6 in each case). Thus, one can measure an important aspect of intelligence directly and without heavy reliance on achievement, rather than indirectly and with heavy reliance on past achievement (Powell & Sternberg, 1982).

Consider second another common type of intelligence test—arithmetic word problems (and at higher levels, algebra and geometry word problems as well). Again, performance on such problems is heavily dependent upon one's mathematical achievements, and indeed, opportunities. Can one measure the main skills tapped by such tests without creating what is essentially an achievement test? We believe we have done so through the insight problems mentioned earlier. Consider two typical examples of such problems:

1. If you have black socks and brown socks in your drawer, mixed in the ratio of 4 to 5, how many socks will you have to take out to make sure of having a pair the same color?

2. Water lilies double in area every twenty-four hours. At the beginning of the summer there is one water lily on a lake. It takes sixty days for the lake to become covered with water lilies. On what day is the lake half covered?

Solutions of problems such as these requires a fair amount of insight, but very little in the way of prior mathematical knowledge.[1] In most problems such as these, a common element in successful solution is selective encoding—knowing what elements of the problems are relevant to solution and what aspects are irrelevant. And performance on such problems is correlated .66 with IQ. Thus, it is possible to use word problems that are good measures of intelligence, but that require very little in the way of prior arithmetical knowledge (Sternberg & Davidson, 1982). Moreover, it is unnecessary to time problem administration. As mentioned earlier, higher performance is associated with more, not less, time spent on the problems.

To summarize: We need not measure intelligence as last year's achievement. It is probably impossible to rid intelligence tests of achievement load entirely. Indeed, it may not even be desirable to do so. But the load can be substantially reduced by asking oneself what intellectual skills one wishes to measure, and then seeking to measure these directly through the use of items that tap the skills rather than their byproducts.

Dubious Assumption #3: Testing needs to be conducted in a stressful, anxiety-provoking situation. Few situations in life are as stressful as the situation confronting the examinee about to receive (and then receiving) a standardized test. Most examinees know that the results of the test are crucial for the examinees' future, and that one to three hours of testing may have more impact on the future than years of school performance. The anxiety generated by the testing situation may have little or no effect on some examinees, and even a beneficial effect on other examinees. But there is a substantial proportion of examinees—the test anxious—whose anxiety will cripple their test performance, possibly severely. Moreover, because the anxiety will be common to standardized testing situations (although often not to other testing situations), the error in measurement resulting from a single testing situation will be compounded by error in measurement in other testing situations. With repeated low scores, a bright but test-anxious individual may truly appear to be stupid. What is needed is some kind of standardized assessment device that is fair to the test-anxious, as well as to others, and that does not impose a differential penalty on individuals as a function of a form of state anxiety that may have no counterpart in situations other than that of standardized testing. I believe that we have at least two promising leads in this direction.

The first lead is testing based on the notion of intelligence as in part a function of a person's ability to profit from incomplete instruction (Resnick & Glaser, 1976). A measure of this ability is now provided by Feuerstein's (1979) Learning Potential Assessment Device (LPAD), which, although originally proposed as an assessment device for retarded performers, can be used for performers at varying levels of performance, including advanced ones. The device involves administration of problems with graded instruction. The amount of instruction given depends upon the examinee's needs. Moreover, the test is administered in a supportive, cooperative atmosphere, where the examiner is actually helping the examinee solve problems, rather than impassively observing the examinee's success or failure. The examiner does everything he or she can do to allay anxiety (rather than to create it!) Feuerstein has found that children who are cowed by and unable to perform well on regular standardized tests can demonstrate high levels of performance on his test. Moreover, their performance outside the testing situation appears better to be predicted by the LPAD than by conventional intelligence tests (see Feuerstein, 1979).

The second lead is based on the notion that intelligence can be measured with some accuracy by the degree of resemblance between a person's behavior and the behavior of the "ideally" intelligent individual (see Neisser, 1979). Sternberg et al. (1981) had a group of individuals rate the extent to which each of 250 behaviors characterized their own behavioral repertoire. A second group of individuals rated the extent to which each of the 250 behaviors characterized the behavioral repertoire of an "ideally intelligent" person. The investigators then computed the correlation between each person's self-description and the description of the ideally intelligent person (as provided by the second group of individuals). The correlation provided a measure of degree of resemblance between a real individual and the "ideally intelligent" individual. The claim was that this degree of resemblance is itself a measure of intelligence. The facts bore out the claim: The correlation between the resemblance measure and scores on a standard IQ test was .52, confirming that the measure did provide an index of intelligence as it is often operationally defined. And doing self-ratings involved minimal stress.

The behaviors that were rated had previously been listed by entirely different individuals as characterizing either "intelligent" or "unintelligent" persons. The intelligent behaviors were shown (by factor analysis) to fall into three general classes: problem-solving ability (e.g., "reasons logically and well," "identifies connections among ideas," and "sees all aspects of a problem"); verbal ability (e.g., "speaks clearly and articulately," "is verbally fluent," and "reads with high comprehension"); and social competence (e.g., "accepts others for what they are," "admits mistakes," and "displays interest in the world at large"). (No attempt was made to classify the unintelligent behaviors, which were not the object of interest in the study.)

I would not propose the behavioral checklist, or the LPAD, for that matter, as replacements for standard intelligence tests. Certainly, there is not enough validity information yet to make such a proposition. But I think that they deserve to be considered as supplements to standard tests. They are much less stress-provoking than standard intelligence tests, and may well be more accurate, at least for individuals who fall to pieces when confronted with standardized tests. Persons who scored high on these new indices but low on conventional indices would merit further follow-up before writing them off as weak or even average performers. Such measures carry the potential of identifying gifted individuals who are being lost for no reason other than their high levels of test anxiety.

Dubious Assumption #4: Precision is tantamount to validity. There is a certain allure to exact-sounding numbers. An IQ score of 119, an SAT score of 580, a creativity score in the 74th percentile all sound very precise. Indeed, social psychologists have found that people tend to weigh accurate-sounding information highly, almost without regard to its validity (see Nisbett & Ross, 1980). But the appearance of precision is no substitute for the fact of validity. Indeed, a test may in fact be precise in its measurements, but not of whatever it is that distinguishes the gifted from everyone else. IQ tests usually account for between 10 and 25% of the variance in scholastic performance—rarely more. Creativity tests usually account for much less. When more consequential kinds of criteria are used (success in various real-world pursuits), the degree of relationship is even less than this. Yet, school administrators and teachers blithely go on as though the tests were highly accurate predictors of interesting criterion performances. They may pat themselves on the backs for using *both* intelligence and creativity tests in the identification of the gifted. Yet, I have yet to see any evidence suggesting that the two kinds of tests, even in combination, provide substantial validity in the prediction of interesting kinds of gifted performance (which does not include performance on still other tests of the same kinds!).

I am not saying that the tests are invalid, or that their use should be abandoned. I am saying that in individual cases, they should be used only with the greatest of care. For reasons discussed earlier in the article, the tests may be valid for some individuals, but not for others.

Few people are willing to admit that they are entranced by test scores. When they hear the results of experiments showing that people overvalue precise sounding information of low validity, they tend to think of these results as applying to the other guy. Because of this tendency, I would like to offer a few anecdotes to back up my claim.

When I worked one summer at The Psychological Corporation, distributors of the Miller Analogies Test (a widely-used test for graduate admissions and financial aid decisions), we heard what I considered then, and still consider, to be an amazing story.

A teacher's college in Mississippi required a score of 25 on the Miller for admissions. The use of this cutoff was suspect, to say the least, since 25 represents a chance score on the test. (There are 100 items with four answer options per item, and no penalty for guessing is subtracted for wrong answers.) A promising student was admitted to the college despite a sub-25 Miller score, and went through the program with distinction. When it came time for the student to receive a diploma, she was informed that the diploma would be withheld until she could take the test and receive a score of at least 25. I am pleased to say that she did in fact retake the test and receive the requisite chance score. But I am less pleased with the logic behind the readministration: The predictor had somehow come to surpass the criterion in importance! The test had become an end rather than a means.

I told this pathetic-sounding story to a large meeting of teachers of the gifted, showing them how bad things could be at an isolated teacher's college in Mississippi. Afterward, a teacher came up to me and told me an essentially identical story (except for a higher cutoff score) as it pertained to her and a very reputable university in southern Connecticut.

That variants of this kind of logic are not limited to isolated cases is shown by the fact that I have encountered personally, and heard about innumerable times, similar experiences at major universities. Consider, for example, the cases of applicants to graduate (and often, undergraduate) programs with stellar credentials except for reduced test scores. In my experience, these applicants have a way of getting a "full and open discussion" of their full set of credentials, and then of getting rejected. Often, people know in their hearts, right from the beginning of the discussion, that the decision will be negative. The discussion seems to do more to alleviate people's feelings of guilt at going with test scores than to do anything else. These negative decisions are particularly frustrating when the applicants have shown excellent competence at the criterion task (in my profession, psychological research), and yet are rejected on the basis of test scores that are at best highly imperfect predictors of performance on the criterion task. Again, the means becomes the end, and people forget which is the criterion and which the predictor. The test becomes more important than the performance it is supposed to predict. When criterion information is unavailable or scanty, test scores can serve a useful function; when such information is available, however, the tests may be superfluous or even counterproductive. The fact that a test score is (or appears to be) precise doesn't mean that it is any good.

To conclude: Tests work for some of the people some of the time. People are often unaware of, and might be embarrassed by a statistical analysis of, their dependence on the scores. Applied conservatively and with full respect to all of the available information, they can be of some use. Misapplied or overused, they become yet another of the lies we live by.

NOTE

1. Answers to the two problems are (1) 3 and (2) 59.

REFERENCES

Baron, J. Reflective thinking as a goal of education. *Intelligence, 1981, 5,* 291–309.

Baron, J. Personality and intelligence. In R. J. Sternberg (Ed.), *Handbook of human intelligence.* NYC: Cambridge University Press, 1982.

Chi, M. T. H., Glaser, R., & Rees, R. Expertise in problem solving. In R. J. Sternberg (Ed.), *Advances in the psychology of human intelligence* (Vol. 1). Hillsdale, NJ: Erlbaum, 1982.

Feuerstein, R. *The dynamic assessment of retarded performers: The learning potential assessment device, theory, instruments, and techniques.* Baltimore: University Park Press, 1979.

Hunt, E. B. Mechanics of verbal ability. *Psychological Review*, 1978, *85,* 109–130.

Jensen, A. R. g: Outmoded theory or unconquered frontier? *Creative Science and Technology,* 1979, *2,* 16–29.

Jensen, A. R. *Bias in mental testing.* NYC: Free Press, 1980.

Lesser, G. S., Fifer, G., & Clark, D. H. Mental abilities of children from different social-class and cultural groups. *Monographs of the Society for Research in Child Development,* 1965, *30,* No. 4.

Matarazzo, J. D. *Wechsler's measurement and appraisal of adult intelligence.* Baltimore: Williams & Wilkins, 1972.

Mulholland, T. M., Pellegrino, J. W., & Glaser, R. Components of geometric analogy solution. *Cognitive Psychology,* 1980, *12,* 252–284.

Neisser, U. The concept of intelligence. In R. J. Sternberg & D. K. Detterman (Eds.), *Human intelligence: Perspectives on its theory and measurement.* Norwood, NJ: Ablex, 1979.

Nisbett, R., & Ross, L. *Human inference: Strategies and shortcomings of social judgment.* Englewood Cliffs, NJ: Prentice-Hall, 1980.

Powell, J. S., & Sternberg, R. J. Acquisition of vocabulary from context. Manuscript submitted for publication, 1982.

Resnick, L. B., & Glaser, R. Problem solving and intelligence. In L. B. Resnick (Ed.), *The nature of intelligence.* Hillsdale, NJ: Erlbaum, 1976.

Sternberg, R. J. *Intelligence, information processing, and analogical reasoning: The componential analysis of human abilities.* Hillsdale, NJ: Erlbaum, 1977.

Sternberg, R. J. Intelligence and nonentrenchment. *Journal of Educational Psychology,* 1981, *73,* 1–16.

Sternberg, R. J., Conway, B. E., Ketron, J. L., & Bernstein, M. People's conceptions of intelligence. *Journal of Personality and Social Psychology: Attitudes and Social Cognition,* 1981, *41,* 37–55.

Sternberg, R. J., & Davidson, J. E. The mind of the puzzler. *Psychology Today*, 1982, *16*, June, 37–44.

Sternberg, R. J., Powell, J. S., & Kaye, D. B. The nature of verbal comprehension. *Poetics*, 1982, *11*, 155–187.

Sternberg, R. J., & Rifkin, B. The development of analogical reasoning processes. *Journal of Experimental Child Psychology*, 1979, *27*, 195–232.

Werner, H., & Kaplan, E. The acquisition of word meanings: A developmental study. *Monographs of the Society for Research in Child Development*, 1952, No. 51.

7

Myth: The Gifted Constitute 3–5% of the Population

Dear Mr. and Mrs. Copernicus:
We Regret to Inform You . . .

Joseph S. Renzulli

There are certain unavoidable pitfalls that we are bound to stumble into if we accept the belief that giftedness can be defined by 3 to 5% of the normal curve. The first pitfall is the belief that giftedness and IQ are one and the same. (Please note that I said IQ rather than intelligence because most psychometric theorists believe that IQ tests measure only a limited part of the psychological construct called intelligence.) We can plot normal curves using IQ *test scores*, but let us not accept uncritically the conclusion that IQ tests truly measure all of the

Editor's Note: From Renzulli, J. S. (1982). Myth: The gifted constitute 3–5% of the population. *Gifted Child Quarterly*, 26(1), 11–14. © 1982 National Association for Gifted Children. Reprinted with permission.

many factors that result in intelligent or gifted behavior. Whether we are willing to admit it or not, if we accept the 3 to 5% myth, then we will implicitly and operationally[1] also accept the equally unsupportable myth that giftedness and IQ are the same thing.

A second pitfall emanating from the 3 to 5% approach is that we are likely to view "the gifted" as a fixed population, one that always can be preselected for special services. This almost universal practice of preselection effectively closes the door to all other youngsters and says, in effect, that no matter what kinds of outstanding abilities a nonselected individual shows, we will refuse any special program assistance because the student is not one of the prechosen few. Such absolutism in our identification procedures is ironic for a field that prides itself on flexibility of thought and alternative approaches to the solution of problems.

TWO TYPES OF GIFTEDNESS

Anyone who reviews the vast number of research studies dealing with characteristics of gifted persons will inevitably conclude that there are really two types of giftedness. I will refer to the first type as "schoolhouse giftedness" and the second as "creative/productive giftedness." Before going on to describe each type, I want to emphasize that:

1. both types are equally important,

2. there is usually an interaction between the two types, and

3. special programs should make appropriate provisions for encouraging both types as well as the numerous occasions when the two types interact with one another.

Schoolhouse Giftedness

Schoolhouse giftedness might also be called test-taking or lesson-learning giftedness. It is the kind most easily measured by IQ or other cognitive ability tests, and for this reason it is also the type most often used for selecting students for entrance into special programs. The abilities people display on IQ and aptitude tests are exactly the kinds of abilities that are most valued in traditional school learning situations. In other words, the games people play on ability tests are similar in nature to the games that teachers require in most lesson-learning situations. Research tells us that students who score high on IQ tests are also likely to get high grades in school. Research also has shown that these test-taking and lesson-learning abilities generally remain stable over time. The results of this research should lead us to some very obvious conclusions about schoolhouse giftedness: it exists in varying degrees, it can be identified through appropriate assessment techniques, and we should therefore do everything in our power to make appropriate modifications for students who have the ability to cover regular curricular material at advanced rates and levels of understanding. Curriculum compacting and other acceleration techniques should represent an essential part of any school program that strives to respect the individual differences that are clearly evident from scores yielded by cognitive ability tests. But let us not forget that IQ scores correlate only from .40 to .60 with school grades. The tests, therefore, account for only 16 to 36% of the variance between these two indicators of potential. Many youngsters who are moderately below the top 3 to 5% in measured ability clearly have shown that they can do advanced level work. To deny them this opportunity would be analogous to *forbidding* a youngster from trying out for the basketball team because he or she missed the "cut-off height" by a few inches! Basketball coaches are not foolish enough to establish *inflexible* cutoff heights because they know that such an arbitrary practice will cause them to overlook the talents of youngsters who may overcome slight limitations in inches with other abilities such as drive, speed, team work, ball handling skills and perhaps even the ability and motivation to outjump taller persons who are trying out for the team. As educators of gifted and talented youth, we can undoubtedly take a few lessons about flexibility from coaches!

Creative/Productive Giftedness

If scores on IQ tests and other measures of cognitive ability only account for a limited proportion of the common variance with school grades, we can be equally certain that these measures do not tell the whole story when it comes to making predictions about creative/productive giftedness. Before defending this assertion with some research findings, let us briefly review what is meant by this second type of giftedness, the important role that it should play in programming, and therefore, the reasons we should attempt to assess it in our identification procedures—even if such assessment causes us to look below the top 3 to 5% on the normal curve.

Creative/productive giftedness describes those aspects of human activity and involvement where a premium is placed on the development of original material and/or products that are purposefully designed to have an impact upon one or more target audiences. Learning situations that are designed to promote creative/productive giftedness emphasize the use and application of information (content) and thinking processes in an integrated, inductive, and real-problem-oriented manner. The role of the student is transformed from that of a learner of prescribed lessons to one in which she or he uses the modus operandi of a firsthand inquirer. This approach is quite different from the development of lesson-learning giftedness which tends to emphasize deductive learning, structured training in the development of thinking processes and the acquisition, storage, and retrieval of information.

Why is creative/productive giftedness important enough for us to question the "tidy" and relatively easy approach that traditionally has been used to select the top 3 to 5%? Why do some people want to rock the boat by challenging a conception of giftedness that can be conveniently defined and easily measured? The answers to these questions are simple and yet very compelling. History tells us that it has been the creative and productive people of the world, the producers rather than consumers of knowledge, the reconstructionists of thought in all areas of human endeavor, that have become recognized as "truly gifted" individuals. History does not remember persons who merely scored high on IQ tests and/or learned their lessons well.

If we could prove that all (or even most) creative producers scored in the top 3 to 5% on the normal curve there would be no justification for the argument being presented here. But let us examine what some of the research tells us about highly creative and productive people and perhaps we can make a case for (a) expanding the range of test scores used in identification and (b) including other forms of information in the identification process.

Cox (1926) conducted an extremely comprehensive study in which she and four other persons (including Lewis Terman) estimated the IQs of 282 well-known 19th century persons. Listed below are the names of only a few of the persons who would *not* have been included in a gifted program if we set the IQ cutoff score at 130:

Cervantes	Lavoisier	Jenner
Copernicus	DeFoe	Lincoln
Faraday	Fielding	Linnaeus
Raphael	Harvey	Locke
Rembrandt	Ben Johnson	Swift
Luther	Haydn	Madison
Goldsmith	Bach	LaFontaine

In a study of the relationship between the contributions of physicists and biologists (based on such criteria as patents granted and the number of publications), Harmon (1963) found that individuals receiving high ratings as professional scientists could not be predicted from any of the academic proficiency information. He also discovered that for nearly half of the correlations computed, the direction of the relationship between these traditional measures of academic success and professional accomplishments was negative. In two studies of professional mathematicians, Helson (1971), and Helson and Crutchfield (1970) found no significant IQ score differences between mathematicians judged by their peers as performing particularly good research and a control group of low productive mathematicians. There were, however, differences between the groups on a variety of personality measures purporting to assess proclivities for creative behavior. Similar results have been reported in studies of chemists and mathematicians (Bloom, 1963), psychologists (Marston, 1971), research scientists (MacKinnon, 1968), artists (Barron, 1963), and architects (MacKinnon, 1968).

In an extremely comprehensive review of occupational studies dealing with traditional indicators of academic success and postcollege performance, Hoyt (1965) concluded that traditional assessments of academic success have at best a modest correlation with various indicators of success in the adult world. The review included forty-six studies in seven occupational areas including business, teaching, engineering, medicine, scientific research, journalism, government, and the ministry. The criteria for determining the level of accomplishment varied from salary level to numbers of publications to behavioral performance ratings. Hoyt asserted that sufficient evidence had been aggregated to warrant a conclusion that "there is good reason to believe that academic achievement (knowledge) and other types of educational growth and development are relatively independent of each other" (p. 73). Similar conclusions were reached in analogous studies conducted by Ghiselli (1973), Creagar and Harmon (1966), and Baird (undated paper).

A study conducted by the American College Testing (ACT) Program titled, *Varieties of Accomplishment After College: Perspectives on the Meaning of Academic Talent* (Munday & Davis, 1974), resulted in the following conclusion:

> The adult accomplishments were found to be uncorrelated with academic talent, including test scores, high school grades, and college grades, However, the adult accomplishments were related to comparable high school non-academic (extra curricular) accomplishments. This suggests that there are many kinds of talents related to later success which might be identified and nurtured by educational institutions (abstract).

In summary, there is a substantial body of evidence which suggests that measures of intellectual or academic potential be used only for initial screening purposes or to establish minimum performance levels, and that greater use be made of indicators of creative thinking, ratings of past accomplishments, and ratings of creative production. Wallach (1976) strongly supported placing more emphasis on work samples as evidence of creative productivity. Hoyt (1965) suggested that greater reliance be placed on "profiles of student growth and development" rather than traditional means of determining academic success. His plea is not to lower standards but to individualize them more by developing checklists of accomplishments that can be indications of a number of things which students can do, and do frequently to demonstrate their potential.

The studies reported also raise some basic questions about the use of tests in making selection decisions. McClelland (1973) has pointed out that tests have tremendous power over the lives of young people and they have been especially efficient devices for screening out Black, Spanish speaking, and other minority group members. To quote McClelland:

Why should intelligence or aptitude tests have all this power? What justifies the use of such tests in selecting applicants for college entrance or jobs? On what assumptions is the movement based? They deserve careful examination before we go on rather blindly promoting the use of tests as instruments of power in the lives of many Americans. (p. 1)

These studies represent only a small part of a large body of research that has been summarized elsewhere (See Renzulli, Reis, & Smith, 1981). The full range of research addresses a question that helps to clarify the issue: if IQ or ability scores cannot by themselves account for high levels of creative/productive giftedness, what other factors must be taken into account? The research tells us that creativity and task commitment are equally important characteristics in the making of a gifted person; and that these two additional types of abilities can be identified effectively when included in a more flexible identification system. What is even more important from an educational programming perspective is that high levels of creativity and task commitment can be developed in students who fall somewhat below the sanctimonious 3 to 5%. To deny youngsters an opportunity to develop high levels of interest, involvement, expressiveness, and advanced level productivity because they missed an arbitrary and indefensible cutoff point is nothing short of educational hypocrisy.

As was the case with schoolhouse giftedness, the research leads us to some obvious conclusions about creative/productive giftedness: it exists in varying degrees, it can be identified through appropriate assessment techniques, and we should therefore do everything in our power to make appropriate modifications for students who have the ability to engage in high levels of creative and productive endeavor. And let us not forget that the greatest payoff for both the individual and for society has come from persons who realized their potential in creative/productive ways rather than through mere lesson learning.

Pay Off Research

In a series of research studies recently completed at the University of Connecticut (Reis, 1981) the quality of student productivity between two groups was compared. One group consisted of subjects that scored in the top 5%, as traditionally measured by tests of academic ability. The second group consisted of students who scored in the top 15 to 20% below the top 5%. This second group would not ordinarily have been eligible for services; however, they were allowed to participate in the gifted program (on an equal basis with the first group) due to the greater flexibility allowed by the Revolving Door Identification Model. The results of the research showed that there were no significant differences between the two groups on 15 measures of product quality. The most obvious conclusions that can be drawn from this research is that high levels of creative productivity can be achieved by students below the top 5% if we use a more flexible identification process and if we emphasize creative/productive giftedness as well as schoolhouse giftedness in our programming models.

Let us end our discussion about the 3 to 5% myth on a more positive note. The abilities that cause youngsters to fall into the highest ranges of the normal curve are important, and by including these students in our gifted programs we have been serving an appropriate part of the gifted population. But the evidence clearly tells us that there are other youngsters who are equally capable of high levels of accomplishment in both types of giftedness. Research, experience, and plain old common sense also tell us something that is undeniably important about students who are well above average in ability. *The greatest gift of all is the person's desire to create and produce. It is what we as teachers do to help stimulate and fulfill this desire that ultimately will determine if we are really worthy of being called teachers of the gifted.*

NOTE

1. By operationally, I mean that we will use IQ tests not only to define giftedness, but also to make decisions about who is accepted and rejected for programs that are designed to develop gifted behaviors in young people.

REFERENCES

Baird, L. L. The relationship between academic ability and high level accomplishment: Academic intelligence and creativity re-examined. Princeton, NJ: Educational Testing Service, undated paper.

Barron, F. *Creativity and psychological health.* Princeton, NJ: Van Nostrand, 1963.

Bloom, B. S. Report on creativity research by the examiner's office of the University of Chicago. In C. W. Taylor & F. Barron (Eds.), *Scientific creativity: Its recognition and development.* NYC: John Wiley & Sons, 1963.

Cox, C. C. The early mental traits of three hundred geniuses. In L. M. Terman (Ed.), Genetic studies of genius, vol. II. Stanford, CA: Stanford University Press, 1926.

Creagar, J. A., & Harmon, L. R. On-the-job validation of selection variables. National Academy of Sciences-NCR, Technical Report No. 26, 1966.

Crutchfield, R. S. Conformity and creative thinking. In H. W. Gruber, G. Terrell, & M. Wertheimer (Eds.), *Contemporary approaches to creative thinking.* Prentice-Hall, 1962.

Ghiselli, E. E. The validity of occupational selection tests. *Personal Psychology,* 1973, 26, 1–36.

Harmon, L. R. The development of a criterion of scientific competence. In C. W. Taylor and F. Barron (Eds.), *Scientific creativity: Its recognition and development.* NYC: John Wiley & Sons, 1963, 44–52.

Helson, R. Women mathematicians and the creative personality. *Journal of Consulting and Clinical Psychology,* 1971, 36, 210–20.

Helson, R., & Crutchfield, R. S. Mathematicians: The creative researcher and the average Ph.D. *Journal of Consulting and Clinical Psychology,* 1970, 34, 250–257.

Hoyt, D. P. *The relationship between college grades and adult achievement: A review of the literature:* Iowa City: American College Testing Program Research Report No. 7, 1965.

MacKinnon, D. W. Selecting students with creative potential. In P. Heist (Ed.), *The creative college student: An unmet challenge*. San Francisco: Jossey-Bass, 1968, 101–116.

Marston, A. R. It is time to reconsider the graduate record examination. *American Psychologist*, 1971, *26*, 653–655.

McClelland, D. C. Testing for competence rather than for 'intelligence'. *American Psychologist*, 1973, *28*, 1–14.

Munday, L. A., & Davis, J. C. *Varieties of accomplishment after college: Perspectives on the meaning of academic talent*. Iowa City: American College Testing Program Research Report, No. 62, 1974.

Reis, S. M. An analysis of the productivity of gifted students participating in programs using the revolving door identification model. University of Connecticut, Bureau of Educational Research Report, 1981.

Renzulli, J. S., Reis, S. M., & Smith, L. H. *The revolving door identification model*. Mansfield Center, CT: Creative Learning Press, 1981.

Wallach, M. A. Tests tell us little about talent. *American Scientist*, 1976, *64*, 57–63.

8

The Legacy and Logic of Research on the Identification of Gifted Persons

Joseph S. Renzulli

Marcia A. B. Delcourt

The University of Connecticut

Are we identifying the "truly gifted" student? How should we test the efficacy of our procedures? The authors assess research on the topics of defining and identifying exceptional potential. They propose three alternative criteria to intelligence test scores as the key criterion for identification.

Editor's Note: From Renzulli, J. S., & Delcourt, M.A.B. (1986). The legacy and logic of research on the identification of gifted persons. *Gifted Child Quarterly*, *30*(1), 20–23. © 1986 National Association for Gifted Children. Reprinted with permission.

W hat are the major issues, problems, and potential research designs for conducting studies on the identification of gifted and talented students? Almost every research study dealing with the gifted and talented includes descriptive information about various types of identification procedures; however, studies about the actual effectiveness of the identification process itself have focused almost exclusively on a single research design. This design generally has attempted to evaluate the effectiveness of various criteria for determining who is "really gifted!" At issue in such studies is the almost total use of IQ scores as the ultimate criteria (dependent variable) for evaluating the effectiveness of alternative criteria (predictor or independent variables). This article will examine some of the problems associated with this design and present three other research designs that are potentially valuable in adding to our understanding of the meaning of giftedness. Before examining these designs, however, we will review some of the major problems and issues underlying research on identification.

THE DEFINITION AND CRITERION PROBLEMS

There are two major reasons why identification studies have generally proceeded along such narrow lines. First, the definition of giftedness has been a subject of heated debate, controversy, and change over the years. Second, the availability of alternative definitions and concomitant programming options related thereto has presented researchers with a dilemma in scientific research commonly referred to as the criterion problem.

Problems associated with the definition of giftedness have been well covered in the literature and therefore will only be described briefly in this section. The earlier and more conservative definitions, based mainly on the legacy of Terman and his associates, equated giftedness with high scores. Over the years more liberal definitions (Witty, 1958; Marland, 1972; Renzulli, 1977) helped to expand the concept of giftedness, but these variations on the strict IQ definition also raised issues about subjectivity in measurement, reliance upon human judgment in making decisions about the quality of human performance in nontest situations, and the evaluation of more complex traits such as creativity and task commitment. In more recent years, concern has been expressed about avoiding "hard-core" labeling in favor of practices such as identification by provision (Shore, 1985), open-door programming (Birch, 1984), the use of "action information" in making identification decisions (Renzulli, Reis, & Smith, 1981), and the multidimensional character of giftedness (Jenkins-Friedman, 1982). Also noted is a shift in emphasis from the absolute concept of "being gifted" to the development of gifted behaviors in certain people, at certain times, and under certain circumstances (Renzulli, 1985).

These changes in the conception and definition of giftedness have presented the researcher with a common problem in science known as the criterion problem. The essence of this problem is the absence of an ultimate criterion to which any predictor variable can be compared. The criterion problem stems from the lack of social agreement regarding an external criterion that can be used as a benchmark against which comparisons can be made. In the behavioral sciences, a criterion is almost always based on human judgment about something deemed important or desirable. The validity of a criterion cannot be established by any empirical means, but rather is a matter of the value that one chooses to attach to a particular phenomenon. Since there is no objectively verifiable means for establishing the validity of a value, scientists can never answer definitively questions that will lead to the establishment of a universally accepted ultimate criterion. This problem is not only present in cases dealing with relatively vague and ambiguous concepts such as giftedness, but can also be found in seemingly more precisely measured concepts such as intelligence. Using Rosch's (1975) theory of concepts applied to the meaning of intelligence, Neisser (1979) has concluded that even "the concept of intelligence *cannot* be explicitly defined, not only because of the nature of intelligence but also because of the nature of concepts" (p. 179).

Although the dilemma presented by the definition and criterion problems will prevent us from achieving an ultimate criterion for the determination of giftedness, categorical research on identification is, nevertheless, possible if investigators can state one or more properties in terms of events or behaviors which are desirable and/or capable of being produced (as in the case of experimental studies). This process, known as operationism or the stating of operational definitions, can help to restrict but not eliminate the criterion problem. Ambiguity (i.e., more than one meaning for a given term) and vagueness (i.e., the existence of borderline cases) will always be present. But clarity and rigor in the specification of behaviors and events will at least allow for restricted types of research on identification to go forward. In the four research designs described below, we will see the kinds of trade-offs that take place as a reflection of the clarity and rigor of the definitions employed.

THE TRADITIONAL TEST-SCORE-AS-CRITERION DESIGN

Space does not permit a comprehensive review of identification studies, but examination of a typical study, and variations on the same design, will help to point out the general approach that has been used in research on identification. A brief description of this study will help to place in perspective the major theoretical issues related to research on identification.

The study that we have chosen to use as our example of the test-as-criterion design is the well known research conducted by Pegnato and Birch (1959). In this study, the following seven criteria were examined singly and in combination to determine their efficiency and effectiveness in identifying "gifted" students: teacher judgment, honor roll listing, creativity in art or music (as determined by the judgment of art or music teachers), student council membership, superiority in mathematics (determined by mathematics teacher judgment), group intelligence test scores, and group achievement test scores. "Giftedness" was defined as a score of 136 or higher on the *Stanford-Binet Intelligence Scale*.[1]

Over the years, several variations on this research design have been reported in the literature, however, the predetermined criterion for giftedness (i.e., high IQ scores) has remained essentially the same.

Some of the variations on this design include the use of a different or broadened range of predictors. When Feldhusen, Baska and Womble (1981) examined a multiple criterion approach, all data were converted to standard scores for ease of comparison. Another statistical procedure, multivariate analysis, is described by Glasnapp et al. (1981) and the additive or weighted matrix approaches (Baldwin, 1978; Weber & Battaglia, 1985) were used to condense information to facilitate classification. High IQ scores have also been compared with characteristics of special populations (i.e., age, sex, socioeconomic or ethnic status) or the focus has shifted to an examination of specific abilities such as creativity (Rimm, Davis, & Bien, 1982). Other studies (Brown & Yakimowski, 1985) have presented subtest score patterns on instruments such as the *Wechsler Intelligence Scale for Children*. In most cases these studies have attempted to "second guess" IQ scores and in some cases experimental treatments such as teacher training in rating procedures (Gear, 1975) have been introduced as interventions.

The major problem with this design is that tests, which traditionally have been used as predictors of performance, have themselves become the criterion. Sternberg (1982) recounts an example that illustrates problems associated with this approach. A given cut off score was required for admission to a particular program, but through an error in the selection procedure, a student without the requisite score was admitted. The student completed the program with distinction but was informed upon graduation that she could not receive a diploma unless she retook the entrance examination and achieved an appropriate score. The logic (or lack thereof) in this case is that "the predictor had somehow come to surpass the criterion in importance! The test had become an end rather than a means" (Sternberg, 1982, p. 160).

In view of the various conceptions of giftedness cited above, and the now almost universal agreement (Sternberg & Davidson, 1986) that giftedness, or the display of gifted behaviors, which is our preferred way of dealing with the concept, is dependent upon traits that include but are not restricted to traditional intelligence measures, we can now examine the Pegnato and Birch study and other similar studies in another way. If one has even the slightest belief that giftedness includes more than traditionally measured intelligence, then the more logical conclusion that one can draw from the Pegnato and Birch study is that predictor variables such as teacher judgments are not good "second guessers" of IQ scores. And this finding can now be interpreted in a much more favorable way so far as alternative criteria are concerned. In our efforts to identify students for participation in special programs, it is valuable to have procedures for examining traits that cannot easily be discerned through the use of traditional intelligence, achievement, and aptitude tests. In other words, the value of alternative criteria increases *because* they do not correlate highly with intelligence.

PERFORMANCE-BASED RESEARCH DESIGNS

There are at least three alternative research designs that use various types of performance (as opposed to test scores) as a criterion for determining the appropriateness of identification procedures. These types of performance exist on a continuum that might best be described as objective to subjective so far as evaluation is concerned. The use of each performance criterion is characterized by certain advantages and disadvantages.

Performance Criterion I: Academic Mastery in a Domain Specific Area

Perhaps the best example of research in this category is the *Study of Mathematically Precocious Youth* conducted at Johns Hopkins University. Stanley (1984) has operationally defined giftedness as the ability to perform at a high level in above-grade-level courses in mathematics. Using tests of mathematical aptitude, he has shown that we can in fact predict with a high degree of accuracy those students who can attain desirable performance levels in mathematics. The beauty of this research design is the strong relationship between the test and the desired performance, and the relative rigor with which *both* the predictor and the desirable performance in mathematics classes can be stated. The criterion, expressed in terms of content mastery, can be objectively evaluated by mathematics teachers, and these evaluations are seldom influenced by the age of the student, the values of the teacher, or the passage of time.

Let us now examine this design in a hypothetical situation in which the definition of giftedness has been expanded to include elements of creativity or originality. This addition would seem reasonable and logical to many theorists because persons who have been designated as gifted by society-at-large have almost always earned this recognition based on the originality of their contributions. The academic mastery as criterion design might now lose some of its power. Although the inclusion of originality meets the condition of events which are desirable and capable of being produced, the originality of contributions, even in a domain specific area, is always more difficult to determine than assessing mastery of a specified body of content.

Performance Criterion II: Creative Productivity in Domain Specific or Interdisciplinary Areas

In research conducted by Reis and Renzulli (1982) action information was used as a predictor of performance criteria that consisted of the development of advanced level products in single or interdisciplinary areas. Action information is analogous to the concept of situational testing and involves placing students in learning situations and evaluating the ways in which they react to the generally open-ended enrichment experiences to which they are exposed. The nature and extent of student reactions are evaluated by both teacher judgment and the student's interest and willingness in pursuing advanced level follow-up activities based on the stimulus situation. An instrument entitled *The Student Product Assessment Form* was used to gauge the quality of students' products. This instrument provides individual ratings for eight specific qualitative characteristics of products and for seven factors related to overall product quality. Evaluations were provided by persons with expertise in the various domains in which products were completed. In this design, a major concern is the extent to which students displayed gifted behaviors in the process of product completion.

Although this design takes into account a broader range of traits associated with behaviors which are desirable and capable of being produced, it is quite obviously more dependent upon professional judgment at both the predictive or identification end of the process, and at the final stage during which student productivity is being evaluated. The reliability and validity of *The Student Product Assessment Form* have been found to be very high (Reis, 1981), however, we must question whether or not these evaluations can be carried out as precisely as the grades rendered by instructors in those cases where performance in a course is the criterion. In courses such as mathematics, where accuracy and precision can be measured objectively, it is safe to conclude that objectivity in measurement will be achieved. But in courses where teachers must render judgments about student themes, creative writing assignments, and levels of classroom participation, it is also reasonable to assume that the same kinds of judgments as those used in Performance Criterion II are being used. In addition to teacher judgments, self and peer evaluations are also included in Performance Criterion II. This is described by studies identifying student characteristics such as leadership (Friedman, Jenkins-Friedman, & Van Dyke, 1984). It should be noted that leadership "performance" in this particular study was based upon ratings of observed student behaviors.

Thus, in certain subject areas or regarding specific student characteristics, we see a good deal of similarity between research designs using Performance Criterion I and II. In both of these designs we also note that there is a more logical and direct relationship between the predictor and the criterion. Both designs side step the issue of trying to predict who is "truly gifted" in the absolute sense. In other words, giftedness is not viewed as possession of a golden chromosome on the parts of certain individuals that need only be discovered through the right combination of assessment techniques. Rather, both designs seek to examine the potential that certain individuals may have for the development of gifted behaviors.

Performance Criterion III: Long Range Creative Productivity

None of the designs described thus far have the power to tell us if our predictor variables will determine those persons who later historians will judge as being the gifted writers, mathematicians, artists and future leaders. If these types of long range productivity are invoked as the ultimate criterion for "giftedness," then research designs that employ long term follow-up of individuals identified at earlier ages must be used. Although longitudinal studies are always fraught with a host of contamination factors, it is, nevertheless, viewed as a means for achieving external validation to earlier identification efforts.

By way of summary, the four designs described above represent different conceptions of giftedness, and they also imply different ways of providing educational services directed toward the development of gifted behaviors. With the exception of the first design, we believe that each of the performance based research designs holds promise of advancing our understanding of the meaning of the word gifted, whether it be used as a noun or as an adjective. The test-score-as-criterion design has undoubtedly been popular because of its convenience and the tidyness of arbitrarily equating giftedness with certain levels of IQ scores. But the performance-based designs help us to raise important issues about how one uses their intelligence *and other* potentials in situations that require the display and development of gifted behaviors. As one person put it, "I know IQ is important, but you just can't major in IQ!"

NOTE

1. Since teacher judgment did not correlate highly with Stanford-Binet IQ Scores, this study has often been cited as a rationale for questioning teacher judgment in the identification process. We reexamine this conclusion in a later section of this paper.

REFERENCES

Baldwin, A. Y. (1978). The Baldwin identification matrix. *Educational Planning for the Gifted: Overcoming Cultural, Geographic, and Socio-economic Barriers.* Reston, VA: Council for Exceptional Children.

Birch, J. W. (1984). Is any identification procedure necessary? *Gifted Child Quarterly,* 28(4), 157–161.

Brown, S. W., & Yakimowski, M. E. (1985, March/April). *Gifted intelligence scores on the WISC-R: What's different about them?* Paper presented at the meeting of the American Educational Research Association, Chicago, IL.

Feldhusen, J. F., Baska, L. K., & Womble, S. (1981). Using standard scores to synthesize data in identifying the gifted. *Journal for the Education of the Gifted,* 4(3), 177–186.

Friedman, P. G., Jenkins-Friedman, R., & Van Dyke, M. (1984). Identifying the leadership gifted: Self, peer, or teacher nominations? *Roeper Review,* 7(2), 91–94.

Gear, H. H. (1975). Effects of the training program, identification of the potentially gifted, on teachers' accuracy in the identification of intellectually gifted children (Doctoral dissertation, The University of Connecticut, 1975). *Dissertation Abstracts International,* 36, (10-A), 6548–6549.

Glasnapp, D. R., et al. (1981, April). *Use of discriminant analysis in the identification of gifted students*. Paper presented at the Annual International Convention for Exceptional Children, New York.

Jenkins-Friedman, R. (1982). Myth: Cosmetic use of multiple selection criteria! *Gifted Child Quarterly, 26*(1), 24–26.

Marland, S. P. (1972). *Education of the gifted and talented* (Report to the Congress of the United States). Washington, DC: U.S. Government Printing Office.

Neisser, U. (1979). The concept of intelligence. In R. J. Sternberg & D.K. Detterman (Eds.), *Human intelligence* (pp. 179–189). Norwood, NJ: Ablex Publishing Corporation.

Pegnato, C. W., & Birch, J. W, (1959). Locating gifted children in junior high schools: Comparison of methods. *Exceptional Children, 25*(7), 300–304.

Reis, S. M. (1981). *An analysis of the productivity of gifted students participating in programs using the revolving door identification model*. Unpublished doctoral dissertation, The University of Connecticut, Storrs, Connecticut.

Reis, S. M., & Renzulli, J. S. (1982). Case for a broadened conception of giftedness. *Phi Delta Kappan, 63*(9), 619–620.

Renzulli, J. S. (1977). What makes giftedness? Reexamining a definition. *Phi Delta Kappan, 60*(3), 180–184 & 261.

Renzulli, J. S. (1985). The three-ring conception of giftedness: A developmental model for creative productivity. In R. J. Sternberg & J. Davidson (Eds.), *Conceptions of giftedness*. New York: Cambridge University Press.

Renzulli, J. S., Reis, S. M., & Smith, L. H. (1981). *The revolving door identification model*. Mansfield Center, CT: Creative Learning Press.

Rimm, S., Davis, G. A., & Bien, Y. (1982). Identifying creativity: A characteristics approach. *Gifted Child Quarterly, 26*(4), 165–171.

Rosch, E. R. (1975). Universals and specifics in human categorization. In R. Breslin, S. Bochner, & W. Lonner (Eds.), *Cross-cultural perspectives on learning*. New York: Halsted.

Shore, B. M., & Tsiamis, A. (1985, August). Identification by provision: Limited field test of a radical alternative for identifying gifted students. In H. Collis (Chair), *Identification and guidance counseling of highly gifted children*. Symposium conducted at the 6th World Conference on Gifted and Talented Children, Hamburg, Germany.

Stanley, J. C. (1984). Use of general ability and specific aptitude measures in identification: Some principles and certain cautions. *Gifted Child Quarterly, 28*(4), 177–180.

Sternberg, R. J. (1982). Lies we live by: Missapplication of tests in identifying the gifted. *Gifted Child Quarterly, 26*(4), 157–161.

Sternberg, R. J., & Davidson, J. (1986). *Conceptions of giftedness*. New York: Cambridge University Press.

Weber, P., & Battaglia, C. (1985). Reaching beyond identification through the "identiform" system. *Gifted Child Quarterly, 29*(1), 35–47.

Witty, P. A. (1958). Who are the gifted? In N. B. Henry (Ed.), *Education of the gifted*, 57th Yearbook of the National Society for the Study of Education, Part II. Chicago: University of Chicago Press.

9

Problems in the Identification of Giftedness, Talent, or Ability

John F. Feldhusen

J. William Asher

Steven M. Hoover

V alid identification of youth for special educational programs and services is indeed a difficult task. Of course, it is not difficult to find tests which have some established validity to measure human abilities, and to administer these tests to prospective participants in a program. Further, it is not difficult to select some arbitrarily high cut-off point which prospects must attain on each test in order to qualify for the program. These arbitrary activities may be carried out in such a way that the identifiers believe they are using the best of scientific technology, administering valid tests, and using good procedures for the identification of gifted, talented, or high ability youth.

Editor's Note: From Feldhusen, J. F., Asher, J. W., & Hoover, S. M. (1984). Problems in the identification of giftedness, talent, or ability. *Gifted Child Quarterly, 28*(4), 149–151.

In truth, identification procedures are complex, and they raise issues of validity and purpose which are of major concern to thoughtful program directors. These directors often are principally concerned with finding an identification system which has face validity and is sufficiently precise to ward off the complaints of parents who challenge the system if their child fails to be selected for a program. To the parents who complain, the program director simply presents the titles of the prestigious tests used indicating the cut-off levels their children failed to achieve. There may, of course, be little empirical justification for the appropriateness of the tests used nor of the basis for the cut-off levels of test scores. Parents simply take it on faith that the latter are defensible. Unfortunately, most program directors are unable to present any theoretically defensible arguments for their procedures.

Problems in the identification of gifted and talented youth can occur at various points within the identification process. A sound identification process includes five major steps, each of which must be viewed separately in order to determine its validity within the framework of the entire process, These five steps are: 1) defining program goals and types of gifted youth to be served; 2) nomination procedures; 3) assessment procedures; 4) individual differentiation, and; 5) validation of the identification process.

PROBLEMS OF GOALS AND TYPES OF YOUTH TO BE SERVED

In approaching the identification process, program directors should consider the goals of the identification process, the types of talent or ability to be identified, the goals of the program and/or the goals for the youth who will be selected. The goals of the identification process might be to find those youth who have high general ability, g, or who have special talents such as verbal reasoning ability, mathematical reasoning talent, or associational fluency. Thus the types of talent or ability are specified. A goal of the program might be to accelerate the development and achievement of verbal reasoning, mathematical reasoning, or associational fluency in youth who are selected. Another goal might be to give the youth an opportunity to gain new knowledge and cognitive skills as rapidly as their ability will allow. These goals can be based on the assumption that not allowing gifted youth to proceed as rapidly as they are able may destroy their motivation to learn, inculcate habits of working at a slow pace, or generate boredom.

The careful determination of program goals will set the direction for the entire identification process. These goals should be determined from an assessment of the needs of gifted and talented youth within the particular setting. Determination of goals also provides direction in evaluating the students, the program, and the identification process itself. Therefore in order to have a defensible identification procedure, it must be based upon clear and defensible program goals.

PROBLEMS IN THE NOMINATION PROCESS

Once goals for the program have been defined special consideration must be given to the nomination-screening process. The major objective of the nomination process is to find all qualified candidates for the program being implemented. The nomination process may be based on available test scores, checklists, rating scales, and other nomination procedures. When available test scores are used, they should bear a valid relationship to the program goals and the types of ability or giftedness to be served in the program.

Selection of checklists and rating scales presents a particular problem. Few published scales offer substantive evidence concerning validity and reliability. Exceptions are the GIFT rating scales reported by Male and Perrone (1979), the Multi-Dimensional Screening Device developed by Krantz (1978), or the Group Inventory for Finding Creative Talent (Rimm, 1976). Program directors should be cautioned not to attempt to develop their own rating scales unless they have had substantial training in psychometrics. Those who choose to use published instruments should be aware of the need to train teacher-raters in the use of the instruments to assure that terminology and concepts used in the scales are understood clearly. Hagen (1980) offers guidelines for the development and use of rating and nomination instruments. Referring to the rating scales which are available or developed locally, she says, "Most of them are . . . pseudo-psychometric instruments" (p. 26). She concludes, "The total score from rating scales is meaningless and useless . . ." (p. 26). Clearly, there is a great need to improve procedures for the selection, development, and/or use of rating scales in the identification process.

Since the use of nomination and rating scales has become ubiquitous in identifying gifted and talented students, one might hope that not only would the best available scales be selected or that developers would have psychometric competence, but also that corroboration of ratings would be obtained by securing multiple assessments from different points of view. ASSETS is a unique rating procedure, in that ratings on the same set of items are secured from the points of view of parent, teacher, and student (1979). Similarly, securing ratings with the *Scales for Rating the Behavioral Characteristics of Superior Students* (Renzulli, et al., 1976) from three or more teachers, focusing on the same child nominee, should increase the reliability, and hopefully the validity of ratings.

PROBLEMS IN INDIVIDUAL ASSESSMENT

The nomination process should generate a larger number of students than might be accommodated into a particular gifted program later. Therefore, additional testing procedures are necessary to provide reliable, individual assessment and to identify special talents and needs. This next step in the identification process is more than simply "weeding out" those who are not qualified for the gifted program. It should also provide teachers, counselors, parents, and administrators with in-depth information on children to be used to provide better individual programming, both for the student in a special program and for those who remain in the regular classroom.

In selecting tests to use for the assessment process a primary consideration is to find instruments which measure those talents or abilities which are goals of the program. Many pullout/resource room programs are designed for verbally precocious youth; there are many language arts activities. Such programs also focus on creativity, because the students in the program are expected to be fluent, imaginative, or flexible. Thus, program directors may wish to select language arts and reading achievement tests and rating scales which assess creativity and writing skills.

A serious problem with the identification process is often a general, indiscriminate use of tests to identify the all-purpose gifted student, regardless of the nature of the program offerings. There is little value, and even probably potential harm, in such a procedure. Ideally, the identification assessment should yield diagnostic information about the student's special talents, aptitudes, abilities, strengths, weaknesses, and needs. Unfortunately, however, such diagnostic information is of little use in programs which offer one general service for all students in the program. This is often the case of pullout/resource room programs which offer a potpourri of creativity and logical thinking activities and independent study. Such programs assume gifted students are a homogeneous group who can all profit equally from a common curriculum.

It would also be desirable to reconceptualize the identification process and move away from the hereditary based concept of a general, fixed, stable, permanent giftedness, and mental ability and attend to the identification of those youth who are not using or developing the full potential of their superior talent or ability. They have special educational needs which are not being met.

There is also much concern about identification of giftedness and talent among minority, disadvantaged, and culturally different students. Some schools believe that there must be a fixed number of "the gifted" among these groups just as there are in general populations. The orientation in that conception is also essentially a hereditary one which asserts that it is "born in," it is stable over time, and there must be unbiased, culture free tests to find "it." Educators of the gifted might indeed serve all youth better if we were to assume that there are children—white, black, hispanic, oriental, etc.—who have relatively superior talent or ability, which in turn causes them to have educational needs which are not readily met in regular school programs. Therefore, the identification process should be directed toward individual assessment and diagnosis of each individual nominee with the goal of making that educational intervention which is best suited to the student's needs.

Nonetheless, for many programs only a limited number of students can be accommodated. In these situations, effort must be expended to have selection procedures which are valid and reflect the goals of the particular program but which also provide individual assessment and programming to meet the needs of students selected.

A major problem in the identification of gifted and talented youth is the labeling process which often follows. Cornell (1983) has shown recently that while the benefits of labeling may be positive for the youngster so designated, the self-concept of siblings may suffer. There is concern that self-concept of peers might also suffer. Apparently the labeling process alone motivates parents to provide opportunities for the "gifted" son or daughter. However, in multichild families, children who are not identified as gifted suffer some decline in self-esteem. Further, little is yet known about the effect of gifted programs on nongifted youth. Perhaps it would be desirable to place less emphasis on labeling students as gifted and to place major emphasis on devising programs to meet the needs of youth who have special talent and abilities.

PROBLEMS IN INDIVIDUAL DIFFERENTIATION

When programs identify a limited or specified number of students there is again a tendency to identify the general, all purpose gifted student. This is seen in efforts to sum up scores from identification instruments to obtain a single composite index of "giftedness." In that process the diagnostic information is lost and there is a singular concentration on the question, "Is the student gifted?"

There may be some value in summing students' scores from several instruments to determine talent or giftedness for a program area, but often the scores added together represent diverse talents and, therefore, diverse program areas. Using the Baldwin Matrix (1977), one might observe ratings of leadership, creativity, motivation intelligence, math achievement and psychomotor capacity all being summed to get a composite score for giftedness! However, a combination of ratings of the related areas of writing skills, reading achievement, language arts achievement, and verbal intelligence might be used to identify youth for a special program emphasizing the development of writing talent. Test and rating scale information might also be used to make decisions on how well the needs of individual students are being met once they are in a program.

Efforts to combine identification data into composite scores were described by Feldhusen, Baska, and Womble (1981). They noted that scores from dissimilar instruments should not be combined, measures should not have their reliability lowered by reducing the scaling to 5- or 10-point intervals, and attention should be paid to differential weighting of scores. The ideal way to combine scores which are similar is to standardize them by conversion to T-scores and then weight as appropriate.

Once youth are identified, a process of educational differentiation (Tannenbaum, 1983) should begin in which the characteristics, interests, talents, and abilities of identified youth are examined, and appropriately differentiated learning activities are prescribed. Verbally precocious youth might be placed in a pullout program stressing language arts, artistically gifted children in a special art class, and mathematically gifted children into a special mathematics class.

Multiple resources are needed to meet the diverse needs of gifted youth (Feldhusen, 1982). Clearly individual educational programs (IEPs) are needed. The identification process should be used to plan individualized program services.

VALIDATING THE IDENTIFICATION PROCESS

In many schools, once the students for a program have been identified, it is assumed that the task is finished. Such an assumption is not defensible. Program directors must obtain evidence that their identification procedures are working as intended and that they truly reflect the goals of the program. This implies that an evaluation be made to determine the effectiveness of the identification process and its possible modification for future use.

In order to validate the identification process, data must be collected which indicates that the instruments used to identify students do indeed predict success in the gifted program. Correlations of the identification instruments with the criteria of success in the program will indicate if there is accurate identification. However, in order to use correlational analysis there must be criteria upon which to validate the identification-selection-program process. These criteria must reflect the goals of the gifted program. They might include standardized tests, teacher ratings of children on performance in the program, or long term indices of success in later stages of life. Once determination has been made of the relative effectiveness of the identification process, revisions can be made which will increase the validity of the identification process.

In summary the identification process in many programs for the gifted and talented should be reviewed carefully. Underlying conceptions and assumptions may be ambiguous or uncertain. Questions of assessment methods, validity, and reliability should be examined as well. Program coordinators may lack the psychometric expertise to examine and refine their identification procedures, and help may be needed. Schools must handle the awesome business of identification of talent, ability or giftedness in professionally defensible ways. The lives of future leaders are at stake and must be handled with proper diligence and care.

REFERENCES

ASSETS. Holmes Beach, FL: Learning Publications, 1979.

Baldwin, A., & Wooster, J. *Baldwin identification matrix inservice kit for the identification of gifted and talented students.* Buffalo, NY: DOK, 1977.

Cornell, D. G. Gifted children: The impact of positive labeling on the family system. *American Journal of Orthopsychiatry*, 1983, 53, 322–335.

Feldhusen, J. F. Meeting the needs of gifted students through differentiated programming. *Gifted Child Quarterly*, 1982, 26, 37–41.

Feldhusen, J. F., Baska, L. K., & Womble, S. R. Using standard scores to synthesize data in identifying the gifted. *Journal for the Education of the Gifted*, 1981, 4, 177–185.

Hagen, E. *Identification of the gifted*. NYC: Teachers College Press, 1980.

Karnes, F. A., & Collins, E. C. *Assessment in gifted education*. Springfield, IL: Thomas, 1981.

Krantz, B. Multi-dimensional screening device for the identification of gifted talented children. Grand Fork, ND: Bureau of Educational Research, University of North Dakota, 1978.

Male, R. A., & Perrone, P. Identifying talent and giftedness: Part I. *Roeper Review*, 1979, 2 (1), 5–7.

Male, R. A., & Perrone, P. Identifying talent and giftedness: Part II. *Roeper Review*, 1979, 2 (2), 5–8.

Male, R. A., & Perrone, P. Identifying talent and giftedness: Part III. *Roeper Review*, 1979, 2 (3), 9–11.

Renzulli, J. S., Smith, L. H., White, A. J., Callahan, C. M., & Hartman, R. K. *Scales for rating the behavioral characteristics of superior students*. Wethersfield, CT: Creative Learning Press, 1976.

Rimm, S. B. *Group inventory for finding creative talent*. Watertown, WI: Educational Assessment Service, 1976.

Tannenbaum, A. J. *Gifted children, psychological and educational perspectives*. NYC: Macmillan, 1983.

Wallach, M. A., & Kogan, N. *Modes of thinking in young children*. NYC: Holt, Rinehart & Winston, 1965.

10

Cognitive Profiles of Verbally and Mathematically Precocious Students: Implications for Identification of the Gifted

Camilla Persson Benbow

Iowa State University

Lola L. Minor

Johns Hopkins University

Performance on tests of specific abilities commonly associated with intelligence was contrasted between 13-year-olds identified as extremely precocious (top 1 in 10,000) in either verbal or mathematical reasoning

Editor's Note: From Benbow, C. P., & Minor, L. L. (1990). Cognitive profiles of verbally and mathematically precocious students: Implications for identification of the gifted. *Gifted Child Quarterly*, 34(1), 21–26. © 1990 National Association for Gifted Children. Reprinted with permission.

ability. Such students differ cognitively. Verbally precocious students scored higher on verbal and general knowledge types of tests, and mathematically precocious students scored higher on tests of nonverbal reasoning, spatial ability, and memory. Results from the factor analysis of test scores (excluding memory test scores) yielded three factors: spatial/speed, verbal, and nonverbal. Mathematically talented students had higher scores on the nonverbal and speed factors; verbally talented students had higher scores on the verbal factor. Thus, at least two distinct forms of giftedness seem to exist (i.e., verbal and nonverbal). Their evolution, moreover, appeared to follow different developmental paths, consistent with Gagne (1985).

Results from a national survey of school personnel prompted the conclusion that "a labyrinth of confusion" concerning the "giftedness" construct is wide-spread (Richert, Alvino, & McDonnel, 1982). Moreover, Hoge (1988) concluded that serious deficiencies exist in current definitions of "giftedness." Educators often view giftedness as something requiring a label (Guskin et al., 1986). To further our understanding of "giftedness," this paper describes the cognitive profiles associated with two types of "giftedness." Implications of the findings for identification of gifted students is then addressed.

Considerable effort has already been made to develop and refine the giftedness construct (e.g., Dark & Benbow, in press; Feldhusen, 1986; Gagne, 1985; Hagan, 1980; Sternberg, 1981, 1986; Sternberg & Davidson, 1986). Most of this recent work, including some of our own work (Dark & Benbow, in press), has been in the information-processing domain. Yet giftedness, as originally operationalized, emerged out of the psychometric tradition of research (e.g., the work of Terman, Hollingworth, or Guilford). Classifying students as gifted on the basis of cognitive ability test scores is a psychometric procedure.

Using time-honored psychometric methods, Benbow et al. (1983) previously investigated the structure of intelligence of students having exceptional general ability. Results indicated that academic giftedness consists of at least two distinct forms: verbal and noverbal. Moreover, Gagne (1985) suggested that talents in different domains relate to a different mix of cognitive abilities, personality traits, and environmental circumstances. If so, then the cognitive profile of students with exceptional verbal talent should differ from that of those with exceptional mathematical talent. In this study, we compare the structure of intelligence of verbally precocious students with that of mathematically precocious students. Mathematically and verbally precocious students' performance was contrasted on tests reflecting the primary mental abilities proposed by Thurstone (1938) and others, as well as on two other tests commonly included in cognitive test batteries. In addition, we explored whether boys and girls selected by the same ability criterion differ in their underlying patterns of specific cognitive abilities. If matched boys and girls do differ, this might help explain gender differences in mathematics and science achievement among the mathematically talented (Benbow & Arjmand, in press; Benbow & Minor, 1986; Benbow & Stanley, 1982).

A secondary purpose of this study was to provide data that might help the practitioner in the identification process. Currently, the "state of the art of identification of gifted and talented youth is in some disarray" (Richert, Alvino, & McDonnel, 1982). Standardized achievement tests and tests of general intelligence are widely used for identification (Yarborough & Johnson, 1983). Yet there is prevailing skepticism that results from either form of assessment adequately reflect giftedness (Feldhusen, 1989). The validity of one overall indicator of intellectual functioning (e.g., the IQ score) has been questioned (e.g., Feldhusen, 1989; Feldhusen, Asher, & Hoover, 1984; Gagne, 1985; Gardner, 1983; Parke, 1989; Renzulli, 1984; Stanley, 1984b; Sternberg & Davidson, 1986). In its stead, a multiple-talent approach has been offered (e.g., Gagne, 1985; Gardner, 1983). Our study provides data assessing the usefulness of this approach.

Putting the Research to Use

The construct of giftedness was investigated. Results indicated that two types of giftedness, verbal and nonverbal, are distinct from one another. Thus, procedures for identifying gifted students should include assessments of both types of talents. Several investigators (e.g., Feldhusen, 1989) have reported that selecting students for a "gifted" program on the basis of one overall ability is indeed questionable. Our results indicated that reliance on global indicators of intellectual functioning may exclude too many nonverbally gifted students, who appear to be less balanced than verbally gifted students in their cognitive development. Gifted students should be selected, therefore, for special programs on the basis of having qualities that match the objectives of the program. Conversely, programs should be developed to serve the educational needs of children with either of these types of giftedness.

Finally, the Raven's Progressive Matrices, a test of general ability, is often suggested as a means of identifying gifted students from disadvantaged backgrounds. The appropriateness of its use, however, has not been validated (Richert, 1987). Data on the Raven test was gathered to determine whether performance on the Raven test was more strongly related to mathematical or to verbal precocity or equally to both. Results could help the practitioner in determining appropriate use of the Raven's in identification of gifted students. It was beyond the scope of this paper, however, to determine the validity of Raven's Progressive Matrices for identification of disadvantaged gifted or culturally different youth.

METHODS

Subjects

The Scholastic Aptitude Test (SAT), a test of developed verbal and mathematical reasoning ability of 17-year-olds (Donlon, 1984), is an especially good measure of reasoning among intellectually gifted 12- to 13-year-olds (Stanley & Benbow, 1986). From November 1980 through October 1983 the Study of Mathematically Precocious Youth (SMPY) conducted a national talent search for students who scored at least 700 on SAT-Mathematics before age 13 (Stanley, 1984a). During those three years, 292 such students were discovered. Almost concurrently, the Center for the Advancement of Academically Talented Youth (CTY) at Johns Hopkins conducted a national search for students who scored at least 630 on SAT-Verbal before age 13. CTY identified 165 students. It was estimated that such students represent the top 1 in 10,000 of their age group in the respective abilities. Several students (48) scored at least 630 on SAT-V *and* 700 on SAT-M before age 13.

As a service for the already identified mathematically precocious students, three supplemental cognitive testing sessions were held in May 1981, 1982, and 1983. Another testing session was held in May 1983 for the verbally precocious students identified in CTY's 1983 Talent Search. Thus, only a small number of verbally talented students were tested. The data from these testing sessions were used in this study. A total of 144 students participated: 106 mathematically talented (termed 700M's), 20 verbally talented (termed 630V's), and 18 who met both the verbal and mathematics criteria (termed Doubles). At the time of testing subjects were approximately 13 years old.

Instruments

A battery of tests sufficiently difficult for highly able students was selected to measure several basic aptitudes. An attempt was made to measure those primary abilities proposed by Thurstone (1938) which have been most frequently corroborated by himself and others. Those primary abilities include: verbal comprehension, word fluency, number, space, associative memory, perceptual speed, and general reasoning. We tested these specific abilities, except numerical ability (since SAT-M scores were already available) and word fluency (which seemed unimportant for extremely precocious students in our sample). We added instead a test of mechanical comprehension and a test of language usage, two specific aptitudes often included in test batteries. Test reliabilities approached .9 for the standardization samples and for our sample.

Spatial Ability (Thurstone's Space) was measured by two standardized tests which were designed for adolescents and young adults (Guilford & Zimmerman, 1981) and one experimental test. The Guilford-Zimmerman Spatial Orientation test measures the ability to perceive arrangements of items of visual information in space. The Guilford-Zimmerman Spatial Visualization test requires the cognition of visual transformations. The transformations are changes in location or position, rearrangements of parts, or sustitutions of one visual object for another. Cubes, the experimental test, measures an individual's ability to form and manipulate mental images of objects (Benbow et al., 1983). All three spatial ability tests were highly speeded.

Nonverbal Reasoning (Thurstone's General Reasoning) was measured by Raven's Progressive Matrices, Advanced Set (Raven, Court, & Raven, 1977). This 36-item, untimed test measures a person's capacity to apprehend relationships among meaningless figures and to develop a systematic method of reasoning. Designed to measure "clear thinking," Raven's test is often used for cross-cultural testing (i.e., testing persons with highly dissimilar backgrounds) (Anastasi, 1982).

Mechanical Comprehension was measured by the Bennett Mechanical Comprehension Test, form AA, which was designed to measure the ability of an individual to understand various kinds of physical and mechanical relationships (Bennett, 1940).

Vocabulary and General Information Knowledge (Thurstone's Verbal Comprehension) was measured by Terman's Concept Mastery Test, Form T. It was designed to test Terman's group of gifted subjects *as adults*. It was designed to measure the ability to deal with abstract ideas at a high level (Terman, 1956). Some investigators consider it to be a difficult test of general intelligence and verbal ability.

Memory (Thurstone's Associative Memory) was measured by using the Coding subtest of the Wechsler Intelligence Scale for Children-Revised (WISC-R). It was adapted for group administration with permission from The Psychological Corporation.

Speed (Thurstone's Perceptual Speed) was measured by the Clerical Speed and Accuracy subtest of the Differential Aptitude Test (Form T; Bennett, Seashore, & Wesman, 1974). This 100-item test was designed for students in grades 8 through 12. It tests speed of perception, momentary retention, and speed of response.

Mechanics of English Expression was measured by the Test of Standard Written English (TSWE), which is one of the three parts of the SAT. TSWE has 50 five-option, multiple-choice items to be answered in 30 minutes.

Procedure

Data were analyzed by use of the SPSSX computer program. In comparisons between the verbal and mathematical talent groups, the 18 tested students who met the criteria for both groups were excluded. Because of the unequal N's in the subgroups, the ANOVAs in this study were nonorthogonal. It was decided to retain the nonorthogonal design (because the larger the total N, the greater the statistical power) and follow the four-step procedure outlined by Applebaum and Cramer (1974) for nonorthogonal ANOVAs. In addition, the data for the 112 subjects who had no missing scores[1] were combined, submitted to a factor analysis (principal-axis), rotated, and factor scores computed. Effect sizes (Cohen, 1977) were computed for all t-tests. For comparison purposes, Cohen arbitrarily classified effect sizes as being either small ($d = .20$), medium ($d = .5$), or large ($d = .8$).

RESULTS

Mean scores of the verbally and mathematically talented students, as well as of those both mathematically and verbally talented, for the various specific aptitude tests are shown by sex in Table 1. The mean scores of the examinees were, for the most part, equivalent to those earned by individuals at least five years older. On the spatial orientation test and especially on the spatial visualization test, these 13-year-olds scored above the average of college students. Even more impressive, however, were the scores on the nonverbal reasoning test. Relative to university students in England, this sample of extremely talented students scored at the 98th percentile on the Raven's. The Bennett Mechanical Comprehension Test proved to be slightly more difficult. Even so, the mean score of these students was comparable to the average earned by 12th-grade males. We conclude that these students' nonverbal aptitudes were highly developed.

Results on the verbal tests were similar. On the Concept Mastery Test the students, while still 13 years old, scored slightly better than a special sample of Air Force captains (Terman, 1956). They also knew a great deal of English grammar, as demonstrated by their TSWE scores. On that test they scored at approximately the 80th percentile of college-bound 12th-graders (ATP, 1984). Finally, on the speed test the extremely precocious students scored at the 90th percentile of 12th-graders, and on the memory test their scaled (according to the WISC-R procedure) score was 16; 10 is considered average for their age.

Talent Group Differences

There were differences in pattern of performance between the two talent groups (see Table 1). The mathematically precocious students scored higher than the verbally precocious students on the spatial, nonverbal reasoning, speed, memory, and mechanical comprehension tests. In contrast, the 630V's scored higher than the 700M's on the verbal and general information test and the test of mechanics of English expression. All the differences between the groups were significant by t-tests, except for mechanical comprehension ($p = .08$). Moreover, all the associated effect sizes were large, except for mechanical comprehension (small). The highest mean scores, however, were primarily

Table 1 Performance by Sex of the Three Groups of Extremely Talented Individuals on the Specific Ability Measures

| | Mathematically Talented Students | | | | | | Verbally Talented Students | | | | Mathematically and Verbally Talented Students | | | | | |
| | Males | | | Females | | | Males (N = 13) | | Females (N = 7) | | Males | | | Females | | |
	$\bar{X}$	s.d.	(N)	$\bar{X}$	s.d.	(N)	$\bar{X}$	s.d.	$\bar{X}$	s.d.	$\bar{X}$	s.d.	(N)	$\bar{X}$	s.d.	(N)
Guilford-Zimmerman Orientation	25.3	9.0	(66)	20.4	9.8	(14)	15.6	7.4	17.6	6.0	26.6	11.8	(10)	31.0	7.1	(2)
Guilford-Zimmerman Visualization	24.8	7.7	(66)	20.7	5.0	(14)	18.0	8.2	17.4	6.5	24.0	7.3	(10)	17.5	0.7	(2)
Cubes	24.5	4.0	(91)	23.1	4.6	(15)	15.4	5.2	19.0	5.0	22.7	7.0	(15)	24.0	2.8	(2)
Raven's P.M.	29.2	4.1	(89)	29.9	3.0	(15)	25.9	4.4	25.3	3.9	29.6	3.2	(13)	32.0	1.4	(2)
Bennett Mechanical Comprehension (AA)	37.8	10.3	(90)	32.5	9.1	(15)	33.1	9.2	32.4	9.8	41.7	10.0	(15)	27.5	7.8	(2)
DAT Clerical Speed and Accuracy	62.5	15.1	(66)	69.2	13.1	(14)	47.2	11.0	49.6	8.2	63.3	14.8	(10)	51.5	0.7	(2)
Concept Mastery Test	52.1	16.8	(67)	59.6	26.7	(14)	85.6	11.1	85.3	9.0	93.5	19.9	(10)	84.5	0.7	(2)
Coding	73.6	11.1	(32)	85.4	7.1	(8)	64.8	9.0	68.9	9.0	63.3	2.4	(4)	84.0	1.4	(2)
TSWE	50.2	8.8	(91)	53.5	6.7	(15)	55.6	4.5	55.5	5.0	58.5	2.1	(16)	60.0	0	(2)
Factor 1 (spatial/speed)	.27	(.72)					-1.1	(.70)			.02	(.77)				
Factor 2 (verbal)	-.28	(.81)					.62	(.41)			.99	(.47)				
Factor 3 (nonverbal reasoning)	.107	(.80)					-.67	(.79)			.23	(.87)				

93

Table 2   Rotated Factor Matrix of the Three Factors

	Factor		
	1	2	3
Spatial Visualization	.40		.50
Cubes	.67		
Spatial Orientation	.40		
Mechanical Comprehension			.77
Raven's P.M.			.53
Clerical Speed & Accuracy	.56		
Concept Mastery Test		.74	
TSWE		.77	

obtained by the Doubles: those 18 who met both the verbal and mathematics criteria.

As a check of the above conclusions, a regression analysis was performed for each test with group and sex as the independent variables. As expected, the important independent variable was talent group, which was significant beyond the .001 level for all tests except TSWE ($p < .01$) and the Bennett Mechanical Comprehension (n.s.). The independent variable sex and the sex by group interaction contributed little to the equations and were not significant.

Relationship Among Test Performances

A principal-axis factor analysis of the scores from eight of the tests was then performed. Excluded was Coding, which had been administered to too few students. Moreover, because the sample size was too small, analyses could not be performed separately by sex and group. Three factors emerged; they accounted for 68% of the variance. The factors were then rotated using the Oblimin method. The resulting pattern matrix is shown in Table 2. The first factor loaded on all the highly speeded tests: the three spatial ability measures and the clerical speed and accuracy test (our measure of speed). Cubes had the highest loading, followed by the speed test. Accordingly, the first factor was labeled spatial/speed. The second factor loaded on the TSWE and the Concept Mastery Test. We labeled it as a verbal factor. The third factor loaded on the various nonverbal reasoning tests, especially the Bennett Mechanical Comprehension and Raven's Progressive Matrices. We identified this factor as nonverbal reasoning.

Factors 1 and 3 correlated .41. Three of the four tests that loaded on factor 1 (i.e., the spatial/speed factor) were spatial ability measures, which is usually considered a nonverbal ability (our factor 3). This probably accounts for the relationship between factors 1 and 3. No other substantial correlations between factors were found (i.e., −.02 and .08).

Factor scores were then computed for each individual (Table 1). ANOVAs by group (630V vs. 700M) and sex were then performed on the factor scores.

The analyses showed that, for each factor, talent group was the significant variable ($p < .001$ for the three factors). Sex and the group by sex interaction were not important. The performance of extremely mathematically talented students was superior to that of the extremely verbally talented students on the spatial/speed and nonverbal reasoning factors. For the verbal factor the verbally talented students exhibited higher performance.

Finally, an interesting trend was revealed. The presence of exceptionally high verbal ability appeared to increase the likelihood of the presence of high mathematical ability. Only one of the verbally precocious students had an SAT-M score lower than 500 (the average score of a college-bound 12th- grade male). The reverse was not apparent: high mathematical ability did not seem to indicate concomitantly high verbal ability. Twenty-two students scoring 700 or above on the SAT-M scored below 430 on the SAT-V (the average score of a college-bound 12th-grade male). These results, which were significantly different ($p < .05$), indicate that verbally precocious students may be more evenly balanced in their cognitive profiles than mathematically precocious students.

DISCUSSION

The constuct, giftedness, is poorly defined and understood (Hoge, 1988), a fact which has contributed to existing problems in the way students are identified as gifted (Feldhusen, 1989). It is now believed that giftedness should be viewed as comprised of multiple talents rather than one general ability (e.g., Gagne, 1985; Gardner, 1983; Stanley, 1984b). Is such a view justifiable? We investigated differences in the pattern of special cognitive abilities of extremely verbally precocious students compared to extremely mathematically precocious students. The two forms of giftedness were found to be distinct, a finding which is consistent with viewing giftedness as comprised of several different talents.

Verbally and mathematically precocious students differed in their patterns of cognitive strength on the individual tests and the factors of which those tests are comprised. Not surprisingly, the verbally precocious scored higher on verbal and general knowledge types of tests, and the strengths of the mathematically precocious were in the nonverbal abilities, Moreover, we factor analyzed the scores on the various ability tests to identify the model of intelligence that best fit the data (e.g., a single factor, "g," or multiple talents). Three factors were identified by the factor analysis. They were labeled spatial/speed, verbal, and nonverbal reasoning. These results are somewhat compatible with Horn and Cattell's (1966) crystallized and fluid intelligence model. Crystallized intelligence is heavily dependent on culturally loaded, fact-oriented learning. Tasks highly correlated with this factor include vocabulary and general information. In contrast, fluid intelligence demands little in the way of specific informational knowledge. It reflects the ability to see complex relationships. Our data and those of Benbow et al. (1983) and Pollins (1984) were consistent with such a dichotomization of intelligence or giftedness.

Our results also indicate that speed might be an important component of extreme giftedness. Dark and Benbow (in press; submitted) present evidence indicating that enhanced working memory and speed were components of giftedness, but were more clearly aligned with mathematical than with verbal talent. The data presented in this paper, which were obtained using a psychometric research paradigm, converge with those obtained by Dark and Benbow, who used an information processing approach to investigate the giftedness construct. Enhanced memory and speed appear to be associated more strongly with mathematical than with verbal talent. Further studies are needed to confirm the importance of the speed factor, however. In our study the spatial/speed factor may be artifactual because the spatial tests in our test battery were highly speeded and the spatial/speed and nonverbal reasoning factor correlated highly.

Becker (1989) had found that among mathematically able students spatial ability did not relate to item performance on the SAT-M. In this study, however, we found that mathematical talent was associated with spatial and nonverbal abilities, as did Cohn (1977). Burnett, Lane, and Dratt (1979) and others have presented similar relationships, but among average-ability students.

Gagne (1985) suggested that abilities interact with environmental conditions and personality factors to emerge as talent in a specific domain. In a series of studies, we now have compared these verbally and mathematically precocious students along several dimensions. In support of Gagne's model, we previously found some differences in personality traits (Brody & Benbow, 1986; Dauber & Benbow, in press) and in environmental circumstances (i.e., an emphasis on books and reading; Benbow, 1989). Now we also have identified differences in specific cognitive abilities. Mathematical talent and verbal talent do appear, therefore, to relate to a different mix of cognitive abilities, personality traits, and environmental circumstances.

No gender differences on any of the specific aptitude tests were found, even though several of the measures utilized traditionally exhibit gender differences. Although based on a small sample size of females, these results suggest that when boys and girls are selected by the same ability criteria, their profiles of specific aptitudes are comparable. Thus, contrary to our predictions, it is unlikely that differences in underlying abilities between boys and girls can explain gender differences in mathematics and science achievement among mathematically precocious students.

This study is limited by the small sample size and the extremely rare sample of gifted students tested. The structure of intelligence among gifted students with less exceptional abilities may differ.

Implications for Identification

Our results indicate that giftedness is not a unitary construct. Verbal and mathematical precocity are distinct forms of intellectual giftedness; they are associated with different cognitive profiles. Thus, students should be selected for special academic programs based upon qualities required by that program. Selecting students for a "gifted" program on the basis of one overall ability does not appear justifiable. Evidence presented in this paper suggests that such a procedure might exclude too many nonverbally gifted students from "gifted" programs. Such students are less balanced in their specific abilities and, therefore, may not rank high on an overall or combined index of ability. This point needs further study.

The results in this paper also provide some support for the use of the Raven's Progressive Matrices Test for identification of mathematically gifted students. Raven's test performance was high for extremely gifted students[2] but was more closely aligned to mathematical than verbal precocity. Moreover, Benbow (in preparation) found that Raven's test scores predicted performance of gifted students in fast-paced mathematics classes.

In conclusion, this study provided a unique opportunity to study the cognitive abilities of students selected as being extremely verbally and/or mathematically precocious. The pattern of performance on tests of the specific cognitive abilities commonly associated with intelligence differed for verbal compared to mathematical precocity. This difference provides justification for a multiple-talents approach to identification of the gifted. Gifted students should be selected for special programs on the basis of having qualities that match the intent of the program, not on the basis of one overall ability. In addition, programs for the gifted should be designed to serve the associated educational needs of the two types of giftedness identified in this study.

NOTES

1. In the first testing session (May 1981) a slightly different set of tests was utilized. Thus, the individuals excluded from the factor analysis were almost all 700M males.

2. The SAT is designed to measure reasoning ability. That students scoring high on the SAT also score high on a test of reasoning (i.e., Raven's) corroborates that claim.

REFERENCES

Anastasi, A. (1982). *Psychological testing*. New York: Macmillan.

Applebaum, M. I., & Cramer, E. M. (1974). Some problems in the nonorthogonal analysis of variance. *Psychological Bulletin, 92*, 335–343.

ATP. (1984). *College-bound seniors, 1984–1985*. Princeton, NJ: Educational Testing Service.

Becker, B. J. (1989). Item characteristics and gender differences on SAT-M for mathematically able youth. Under review.

Benbow, C. P. (1989). The role of the family environment in the development of extreme intellectual precocity. Under review.

Benbow, C. P. (in preparation). Factors associated with performance in fast-paced mathematics classes.

Benbow, C. P., & Arjmand, O. (in press). Predictors of high academic achievement in mathematics and science by mathematically talented students: A longitudinal study. *Journal of Educational Psychology*.

Benbow, C. P., & Minor, L. L. (1986). Mathematically talented students and achievement in the high school sciences. *American Educational Research Journal, 23*, 425–436.

Benbow, C. P., & Stanley, J. C. (1982). Consequences in high school and college of sex differences in mathematical reasoning ability: A longitudinal study. *American Educational Research Journal, 19*, 598–622.

Benbow, C. P., Stanley, J. C., Zonderman, A. B., & Kirk, M. K. (1983). Structure of intelligence of intellectually precocious children and of their parents. *Intelligence, 7*, 129–152.

Bennett, G. K. (1940). *Manual for Test of Mechanical Comprehension, Form AA*. New York: The Psychological Corporation.

Bennett, G. K., Seashore, H. G., & Wesman, A. G. (1974). *Manual for the Differential Aptitude Tests, Forms S and T*. New York: The Psychological Corporation.

Brody, L. E., & Benbow, C. P. (1986). Social and emotional adjustment of adolescents extremely talented in verbal and mathematical reasoning. *Journal of Youth and Adolescence, 15*, 1–18.

Burnett, S. A., Lane, D. M., & Dratt, L. M. (1979). Spatial visualization and sex differences in quantitative ability. *Intelligence, 3*, 345–354.

Cohen, J. (1977). *Statistical power analysis for the behavioral sciences*. New York: Academic Press.

Cohn, S. J. (1977). Cognitive characteristics of the top-scoring participants in SMPY's 1976 talent search. *Gifted Child Quarterly, 22*, 416–421.

Dark, V. J., & Benbow, C. P. (in press). Enhanced problem-translation and short-term memory: Components of mathematical talent. *Journal of Educational Psychology*.

Dark, V. J. & Benbow, C. P. (submitted for publication). Differential enhancement of working memory with mathematical and verbal precocity.

Dauber, S., & Benbow, C. P. (in press). Aspects of personality and social behavior in extremely talented young adolescents. *Gifted Child Quarterly*.

Donlon, T. (1984). *The College Board technical handbook for the Scholastic Aptitude Test and Achievement Tests*. New York: College Board.

Feldhusen, J. F. (1986). A conception of giftedness. In R. J. Sternberg & J. E. Davidson (Eds.), *Conceptions of giftedness* (pp. 112–127). New York: Cambridge University Press.

Feldhusen, J. F. (1989). Synthesis of research on gifted youth. *Educational Leadership, 46(3)*, 6–11.

Feldhusen, J. F., Asher, J. W., & Hoover, S. M. (1984). Problems in the identification of giftedness, talent, or ability. *Gifted Child Quarterly, 28*, 149–156.

Gagne, F. (1985). Giftedness and talent. *Gifted Child Quarterly, 29*, 103–112.

Gardner, H. (1983). *Frames of mind*. New York: Basic Books.

Guilford, J. P., & Zimmerman, W. C. (1981). *The Guilford-Zimmerman Aptitude Survey: Manual of instructions and interpretations*. Beverly Hills, CA: Sheridan Psychological Services, Inc.

Guskin, S. L., Okolo, C., Zimmerman, E., & Ping, C. Y. J. (1986). Being labeled gifted or talented: Meanings and effects perceived by students in special programs. *Gifted Child Quarterly, 30*, 61–65.

Hagan, E. (1980). *Identification of the gifted*. New York: Teachers College Press.

Hoge, R. D. (1988). Issues in the definition and measurement of the giftedness construct. *Educational Researcher, 17(7)*, 12–16.

Horn, J. C., & Cattell, R. B. (1966). Refinement and test of the theory of fluid and crystallized ability intelligences. *Journal of Educational Psychology, 58,* 120–136.

Parke, B. N. (1989). Educating the gifted and talented: An agenda for the future. *Educational Leadership, 46 (3),* 4–5.

Pollins, L. D. (1984). The construct validity of the Scholastic Aptitude Test for young gifted students. Unpublished doctoral dissertation, Duke University.

Raven, J. C., Court, J. H., & Raven, J. (1977). *Manual for Raven's Progressive Matrices and Vocabulary Scales.* London: H. K. Lewis & Co., Ltd.

Renzulli, J. S. (1984). The triad/revolving door system: A research-based approach to identification and programming for the gifted and talented. *Gifted Child Quarterly, 28,* 163–171.

Richert, E. S. (1987). Rampant problems and promising practices in the identification of disadvantaged gifted students. *Gifted Child Quarterly, 31,* 149–154.

Richert, E. S., Alvino, J. J., & McDonnel, R. C. (1982). *National report on identification: Assessment and recommendations for comprehensive identification of gifted and talented youth.* Sewell, NJ: Educational Improvement Center-South.

Stanley, J. C. (1984a). The exceptionally talented. *Roeper Review, 6,* 160.

Stanley, J. C. (1984b). Use of general and specific aptitude measures in identification: Some principles and certain cautions. *Gifted Child Quarterly, 28,* 177–180.

Stanley, J. C., & Benbow, C. P. (1986). Youths who reason exceptionally well mathematically. In R. J. Sternberg & J. E. Davidson (Eds.), *Conceptions of giftedness* (pp. 361–387). New York: Cambridge University Press.

Sternberg, R. J. (1981). A componential theory of intellectual giftedness. *Gifted Child Quarterly, 25,* 86–93.

Sternberg, R. J. (1986). *Intelligence applied.* San Diego, CA: Harcourt, Brace, Jovanovich.

Sternberg, R. J., & Davidson, J. E. (Eds.) (1986). *Conceptions of giftedness.* New York Cambridge University Press.

Terman, L. M. (1956). *Manual for Concept Mastery Test, Form T.* New York: The Psychological Corporation.

Thurstone, L. L. (1938). *Primary mental abilities.* Chicago: The University of Chicago Press.

Yarborough, B. H., & Johnson, R. A. (1983). Identifying the gifted: A theory-practice gap. *Gifted Child Quarterly, 27,* 135–138.

11

Screening and Identifying Students Talented in the Visual Arts: Clark's Drawing Abilities Test

Gilbert Clark

Indiana University

Categories of giftedness derived from the influential Marland Report (1972) include students who are gifted in the *visual and performing arts*. The research reported here describes development, testing, and use of a new instrument, Clark's Drawing Abilities Test, and its success in screening and/or identifying students for a visual arts program for artistically gifted students. The test was administered along with the Children's Embedded Figures Test, and the results of both measures subsequently were compared to teacher ratings of students. Significant correlations were obtained among these three measures. Analyses of validity are reported here. Reliability is also reported as expressed in high correlations among test items.

Editor's Note: From Clark, G. (1989). Screening and identifying students talented in the visual arts: Clark's drawing abilities test. *Gifted Child Quarterly*, *33*(3), 98-105. © 1989 National Association for Gifted Children. Reprinted with permission.

There has never been any doubt in my mind that of all the tests and techniques used by psychologists who work with children, there is one that is more meaningful, more interesting, and more enjoyable than all the others and this technique is drawing, just drawing with pencil and paper.

(Koppitz, 1968, p. ix)

A relatively new demand for gifted/talented programs that include students who are gifted in the visual and performing arts has created many problems for school personnel. Screening and identification, one of the major problems, has been very difficult due to a lack of agreed-upon definitions of important terms and a further lack of standardized test instruments. In the research reported here, a new screening and/or identification instrument, Clark's Drawing Abilities Test, is described and discussed. In addition to its use in other research, the test has been used for several years with students attending a visual arts summer institute for artistically talented students. Although a limited number of students have been tested, Clark's Drawing Abilities Test appears to be highly effective as a screening and/or an identification instrument for students who are gifted in the visual arts.

For just over 100 years, measurement and analysis of abilities of children who draw and perform other visual arts–related tasks have consumed the attention of a number of researchers from many parts of the world. Most writers recognize Englishman Ebenezer Cooke's analysis of children's drawings, printed in 1885–1886, as the first major study of children's drawing abilities. Cooke, an English teacher, wrote in London's *Journal of Education*. Soon after Cooke's analysis was published, an Italian, Carrado Ricci, wrote *L'Arte dei Bambini (The Art of the Child)* in 1887. This book, devoted to the study of children's drawings, was followed by a flood of research throughout Europe, England, and the United States. Clark's 1987 review of this extensive literature cited over 190 reported research studies of children's abilities in the visual arts and the use of over 125 different tests to measure various aspects of children's art abilities.

The use of tests to measure visual arts abilities began with the work of Edward L. Thorndike (1913, 1916). Thorndike was concerned that the numerous research studies about children's drawings that preceded his work lacked any standardization of measurement and, in most cases, theoretical bases. His purpose was to create graded scales that teachers could use to evaluate children's drawings and aesthetic choices. Thorndike (1913) described the use of his *Scale For the Merit of Drawings By Pupils 8 to Fifteen Years Old* in this way:

The scale will be of service wherever the merit of the drawings of any child or group of children is to be compared with the merit of the drawings of any other child or group of children or with the drawings of the same child or group of children under other conditions. (p. 17)

Once in place, Thorndike's scale was used by other researchers, such as Childs (1915) and by 1919 numerous tests of drawing and other art abilities were being used in major research projects to help identify and describe gifted/talented students (Whipple, 1919; Manual, 1919). This practice has continued from 1913 to the present, and inquiry about children's art abilities and research using visual arts tests have been reported with great frequency during this time (Clark, 1987). Most of this inquiry has been based upon analyzing and grading children's drawings that had been assigned in various ways.

Putting the Research to Use

Clark's Drawing Abilities Test has been shown to be effective for screening or identifying candidates for a gifted/talented program in the visual arts. The test also is being used to research other questions, such as the assertions that visual arts talent is normally distributed (Clark, 1982) or that visual arts talent and intelligence are highly correlated (Hollingworth, 1923; Vernon, Adamson, and Vernon, 1972). Teachers, program coordinators, and other school personnel may find this test useful in screening and identifying students for participation in any form of visual arts enrichment program. The data presented offer clear evidence for the use of Clark's Drawing Abilities Test in gifted/talented education.

Purpose of This Research

This report will describe several years of development and testing of a new research instrument, Clark's Drawing Abilities Test, based upon a series of drawing tasks, a criteria scale, and an objective scoring guide that has been used in a series of experimental studies. The test has been designed as a research instrument for many purposes, including screening and/or identifying students who are gifted in the visual arts. Even when used in these ways, however, it has not been nor should it be used as the sole basis for accepting or rejecting an applicant to a program for artistically gifted students.

There are aspects of use of this instrument for screening and identification of students gifted in the visual arts that will be reported tentatively at this time pending use of the test with much larger samples and in a variety of other geographic locations. Nevertheless, the findings reported are positive and indicate that this new test is effective in identifying most students with superior abilities in the visual arts.

INSTRUMENT DEVELOPMENT

In 1983 I received a grant to develop an instrument that could be used to test, among other things, the assumption of normal distribution of visual arts–related talent among school age children. Following an extensive survey of uses of the terms *talent* and *talented* in art and gifted/talented education literature and conceptual analyses of the content and tasks used in many instruments and scales that have been used to identify artistically talented students in the past, I decided to limit the instrument to be developed to a few specific drawing tasks. There are extensive precedents for this decision in previous research (Clark, Zimmerman, and Zurmuehlen, 1987).

Stalker (1981) recently used the drawing ability of college age students specifically as a variable to be tested as an identification device for giftedness in art. She reported that drawing ability was *the* most important variable and that it explained most of the variance among other variables in her research project. She claimed that "ability in drawing is fundamental to performative ability and interest in art" (p. 1).

Large numbers of researchers, including Barnes (1893, 1902), Clark (1897), Kerschensteiner (1905), Ivanoff (1909), Rouma (1913), Meumann (1914), Manual (1919), Goodenough (1924, 1926), Tiebout (1933–34), Harris (1963), Eisner (1967), Lewis (1973), Oliver (1974), Wilson and Wilson (1977, 1979), Youngblood (1979), and Silver (1983) have focused their attention upon children's drawings for this and many other reasons:

> Children use drawing primarily as graphic language, as a means of interpreting their thoughts and projecting their ideas in objective form . . . through drawing he is expressing his thoughts and satisfying his need for self expression. (Hildreth, 1941, p. 1)

One reason drawing has been used often is that it is the easiest mode of visual arts expression to assign, administer, and measure; more importantly, it has been recognized as basic to expression in all art forms and as a correlate of many other attributes, including general intelligence (Whipple, 1919; Whitford, 1919a, 1919b; Jones, 1922; Tiebout & Meier, 1936; Lark-Horovitz, 1941; Hildreth, 1941; Munro, Lark-Horovitz, & Barnhardt, 1942; Eisner, 1967; Gutteter, 1972; DiLeo 1973, 1977; Getzels & Csikszentmihalyi, 1976; Goodnow 1977; NAEP, 1977, 1981; Stalker, 1981; Wilson & Wilson, 1982; Van Sommers, 1984). DiLeo (1977) has pointed out, for instance, that:

> With the approach of adolescence . . . drawing will be replaced by other more satisfying forms of self-expression. The gifted will persevere. This decline of interest . . . does not seem to be culturally determined. It has been observed in the youth of many nations. (p. 167)

DiLeo discussed drawing as a particularly apt task for identification of giftedness in the visual arts for young adolescents because their persistence in this form of expression is relatively unique and is, in itself, evidence of possible giftedness. In addition, others have noted that drawing abilities are evidence of skills and knowledge, an assumption that underlies the research reported here:

> The ability to draw well, as to write well, depends not only upon developing skills and increasing awareness of the world but also upon knowledge of the problems of art and artists. (Wilson, Hurwitz, & Wilson, 1987, p. 43)

Drawing Tasks

Major aspects of the development of Clark's Drawing Abilities Test were the selection of appropriate drawing tasks and the construction of a criteria scale and scoring procedure that could be used by various persons when grading drawings made by test subjects. In order to select drawing tasks appropriate to the purposes of the test being developed, four drawing tasks that had been used in one form or another in earlier research studies were adapted. The four tasks and the sources from which they were adapted are: (1) Draw an interesting house as if you were looking at it from across the street (Thorndike, 1913; Whitford, 1919a; McCarty, 1920; Lewerenz, 1927; Lark-Horovitz, 1941), (2) Draw a person who is running very fast (Lewerenz, 1927; Lark-Horovitz, 1941; NAEP, 1981), (3) Draw a picture of you and your friends playing in a school yard (many researchers have collected some type of 'crowd' drawing (Thorndike, 1913; Whipple, 1919; Horn, 1935; Eisner, 1967), and (4) make a fantasy drawing from your imagination (there are literally dozens of researchers who have used a similar task). In addition to the above instructions, each drawing task also included instructions to "use a #2 pencil and make the best drawing you can. Use no more than 15 minutes to complete the drawing." Each drawing is to be completed within 15 minutes. These four tasks, or test items, were considered sufficient to collect salient evidence of general drawing abilities and to measure degrees of difference among their occurrence.

Scoring Criteria and Grading Procedures

Numerous scoring systems have been used to evaluate children's drawings in the past, but many were founded upon highly subjective decisions by judges. This subjectivity has been criticized by many writers (i.e., Eisner, 1972; Barron, 1972; Clark & Zimmerman, 1984). In this test development work, an attempt was made to create as nearly objective a criteria system as possible. In order to do this, a criteria scale and grading system were created based upon observable characteristics of children's drawings although the scale and grading system were derived and adapted from a system of attributes of art works previously used to describe, analyze, and evaluate adult art (Broudy 1972; Silverman, 1982). The major categories used were (1) sensory properties (line, shape, texture value, (2) formal properties (rhythm, balance, unity, composition), (3) expressive properties (mood, originality), and (4) technical properties (technique, correctness of solution). Each of the 12 properties was graded on a 1–5 scale, resulting in a theoretical score range of 12 (one point each) to 60 (five points each). The grading scale resulted in a specific, numerical score for each subject; therefore, students could be rank ordered in terms of their performance on the test. Use of this art work 'property system,' developed by Broudy (1972), served to base the scoring criteria and grading procedures on a popular set of concepts commonly used by many art teachers for other purposes.

SCREENING OR IDENTIFYING STUDENTS GIFTED IN THE VISUAL ARTS

In a series of field tests from 1981 to 1984, Clark's Drawing Abilities Test was used with sets of subjects in various college classes, public school classes, and a summer arts institute for upper elementary, junior high school, and lower secondary school students identified as gifted in the visual and performing arts. Resulting data yielded, at least nominally, normal distributions in each of these field tests. This finding lends credence to the assertion that *talent* in the visual arts is a normally distributed human characteristic, as is *intelligence*. This was the original research problem for which the instrument was developed. When the Drawing Abilities Test was field tested with participants in a summer arts institute for artistically talented students in 1983, it was noted that results correlated very highly with teacher ratings of student performance in the program. As a result, a specific research study was planned to attempt to verify this informal observation.

Methodology

Subjects for this research were all 60 participants in the 1984 Indiana University Summer Arts Institute, an annual two-week residential program for students identified as artistically talented or gifted. The students were to be entering grades 7–11 in the fall of 1984 and were 11–16 years old. There were 31 female and 29 male participants. Most attended from relatively small Indiana communities, but there also were two out-of-state participants. Each participant was recommended to the Institute by teachers and administrators at his or her local school. They were assumed to be artistically talented because their nomination was based upon criteria developed by the Institute staff and communicated to all teachers and parents of possible nominees. These criteria were designed to be 'open-ended,' however, in an attempt to encourage students who may or may not have received art instruction that could develop their unique abilities and to make it possible for students to attend whose art interests may be pursued out-of-school and, therefore, might not be known to their teacher. Many students fit this description (Wilson & Wilson, 1982).

Announcements sent to teachers and parents specified that participants should meet *at least three* of the following criteria: (1) highly interested in one or more of the visual arts, (2) experienced in participating in one or more of the visual arts, (3) highly motivated and self-confident in one or more of the visual arts, (4) achievement scores at least two grades higher than the students' present grade, (5) measured, above-average intelligence, or (6) presently placed in a local gifted/talented school program (Clark & Zimmerman, 1984). The first three are relative and require subjective judgments; the last three are absolute and require access to objective information. It is very common for an application packet to include information from a teacher or parent that an applicant meets five or six of these criteria.

In order to explore validity questions in this research, two measures were administered in addition to the drawing test. These were the Children's Embedded Figures Test (CEFT) (Karp & Konstadt, 1963) and teacher ratings. Teacher ratings were collected by having each teacher in the Institue rank order all students in each class by criteria of successful performance. There were 12 classes offered in the Institute with about 20 students in each class; classes included drawing and painting (three sections), printmaking, ceramics, sculpture, photography, figure drawing (two sections), computer graphics, theater, and dance.

The Children's Embedded Figures Test was administered because a number of researchers have used this instrument in art education research in a continuing search for possible correlations of *cognitive style* with various arts abilities (see Zimmerman (1983) for a review of cognitive-style and visual arts research; Ahmad, 1982; Lovano-Kerr, 1983). High scores on all versions of the Embedded Figures Test require that subjects have a sensitive, high degree of perceptual acuity and are able to differentiate and isolate specific forms within a more complex pattern; many people have speculated that artists, therefore, should score above nonartists on this popular measure. Evidence that this may be true was found in this research.

Feldhusen, Asher, and Hoover (1984) have specified that a major criterion for measurement of success in a program would be "teacher ratings of children on performance in the program" (p. 151).

> In order to validate the identification process, data must be collected which indicates that the instruments used to identify students do indeed predict success in the gifted program. Correlations of identification instruments with criteria of success in the program will indicate if there is accurate identification. (p. 151)

In order to collect such ratings for this research, each of the twelve teachers at the Institute was asked to rate all of his or her students, on a standard form, in categories of *superior, above average, average,* and *below average* in regard to successful performance in class. Each participant attended three different classes and was rated by three different teachers. Each teacher established his or her own criteria of successful performance for each class on the basis of the attainment of objectives established for each class. The painting teacher, a Fine Arts faculty member, set the following objectives for this class. His first objective was to help participants understand how an artist feels by experiencing and sensing their reactions during painting. His second objective was to have them paint an adequate self-portrait. Secondarily, he was concerned with effort, commitment, and attitudes shown in the painting studio. His ratings were based on the attainment of these general objectives and behaviors.

The Children's Embedded Figures Test and Clark's Drawing Abilities Test were administered to students on the first night students arrived at the Institute, before they had attended any classes. The testing was conducted by the author in a large auditorium. Teacher ratings were collected on the last day of classes after teachers had delivered two weeks of intensive instruction and had had many interactions with their students.

Other variables were recorded based upon information reported on students' application forms. These included age, grade in school, gender, and socio-economic status (based upon parents' occupations). All of the variables plus drawing test scores, field dependence, and teacher ratings were coded and the data run in an SPSS multiple correlation program.

Results and Discussion

Relevant data regarding correlations among the variables are shown in Table 1. The most important finding is that scores on each item in Clark's Drawing Abilities Test correlated significantly with teacher ratings of success in this program for artistically talented students. An .05 significance level was used for this research; correlations between the four drawing tasks in Clark's Drawing Abilities Test and teacher ratings of success in their classes were all significant. This finding is consistent with previous findings by other researchers in respect to drawing abilities and other measures (Tiebout & Meier, 1936; Hildreth, 1941; DiLeo 1973, 1977; Gutteter, 1972; Stalker, 1981).

One of the interesting findings of this research is a lack of correlation between age and performance on drawing tasks and teachers' ratings. The Institute staff places students in classes according to student interest as expressed on application forms. As a result, Institute teachers may have up to five years of variance in ages of students in their classes. It has been found that this creates few difficulties and that most age differences disappear when all students are at a relatively high level of performance and working with other students with similar interests and abilities. Negative correlations between two drawing items and subject age and grade indicate that some younger subjects out-performed older subjects on these tasks. Throughout the eight year history of the Institute, numbers of teachers and staff members have observed that some superior younger students often out-perform their older classmates in their art and other class work.

Significant correlation of scores on the Children's Embedded Figures Test with teacher ratings and each of the four drawing tasks on the Drawing Abilities Test calls for an explanation. Scoring of all forms of the Embedded

Table 1 Pearson Correlation Coefficients Among Variables

	Age	Grade	CEFT	Rating	Draw 1	Draw 2	Draw 3	Draw 4
Age		.81*	.29*	.21	.12	−.06	−.07	.06
		$p = .000$	$p = .019$	$p = .070$	$p = .208$	$p = .344$	$p = .321$	$p = .353$
Grade			.19	.24*	.13	−.07	−.07	.15
			$p = .095$	$p = .042$	$p = .177$	$p = .320$	$p = .311$	$p = .145$
CEFT				.24*	.36*	.29*	.27*	.32*
				$p = .046$	$p = .005$	$p = .022$	$p = .034$	$p = .012$
Rating					.34*	.35*	.37*	.39*
					$p = .008$	$p = .006$	$p = 005$	$p = .003$
Draw 1						.73*	.69*	.61*
						$p = .000$	$p = .000$	$p = .000$
Draw 2							.81*	.65*
							$p = .000$	$p = .000$
Draw 3								.71*
								$p = .000$
Draw 4								

$* = > .05$ significant level. $N = 60$.

Figures Test favors subjects who are largely field-independent. Students at the Institute who displayed vastly different styles of expression and working processes (more painterly or designerly or more haptic or visual than other students) but were considered superior by their teachers appeared to score similarly (high field-independence) on the Embedded Figures Test. This finding seems to verify Rouse's earlier (1963) speculation that extremes on Lowenfeld's Visual-Haptic continuum (Lowenfeld & Brittain, 1964) are related to Witkin's field-independent cognitive style. Both predominantly visual and haptic students seemed to be more field-independent; students in the middle (indefinite style) were more field-dependent. *Dissimilarities* between art works of students who scored similarly high scores on the Children's Embedded Figures Test are dramatic. Students with the weakest drawing skills (indefinite style) were those who scored lowest on Clark's Drawing Abilities Test and the Children's Embedded Figures Test (indicating that they were more likely to be field-dependent).

All correlations of the four drawing tasks on Clark's Drawing Abilities Test with one another are significant beyond the .01 level (see Table 1). This high degree of relationship among them was not anticipated; it was an unexpected verification of the power of each of the drawing tasks used in the test and partially explains its effectiveness as a research and/or identification instrument. The author and others who scored the tests had expressed concern that the fantasy drawing task (item 4) would be inconsistent with results on the other three items. This item is 'open-ended' and lacks the specific assignment of content found in other items; in casual examination of completed test booklets it often appears that the fantasy drawings differ in style and content from assigned topic drawings. In scoring, however, there was a significant correlation between performance on this item and the other three drawing tasks.

One aspect of this research had been questioned by colleagues associated with the Institute. They observed that the scoring criteria seem to reward representational or realistic drawings and might, therefore, place students with other, more expressive skills at a disadvantage. This, however, does not appear to be true. One reason is that the age group for whom this test was designed (upper elementary, junior high, and lower secondary students) are at Lowenfeld's (Lowenfeld & Brittain, 1984) stage of *Dawning Realism*. That is, they are at a developmental level where they are consciously and deliberately developing emerging abilities to depict things realistically. Another reason is that high correlations found in this research between scores on the Children's Embedded Figures Test and Clark's Drawing Abilities Test indicate that students with very divergent styles of depiction are rewarded equally by proper use of the drawing test's scoring criteria system.

Subsequent research, including testing participants in the Indiana University Summer Arts Institute in the summers of 1985, 1986, 1987, and 1988, has reinforced all of the findings reported above. Sex and SES variables have been found to lack significance in relationship to the variables of age, grade, Children's Embedded Figures Test scores, teachers' ratings, or performance on the four drawing tasks of Clark's Drawing Abilities Test.

Screening and Identification

During summer sessions in the years after 1984, an effort has been made to critique Clark's Drawing Abilities Test in terms of its success as a screening and/or identification instrument. Swassing's (1985) definitions of *screening* and *identification* have been used in this inquiry:

> Identification is a two-step process: screening and identification. Screening is an initial sorting of all students into two groups: those who are likely to be candidates for the specialized experiences and those who will not be served by the program. Identification is an in-depth examination of the pool of candidates to decide who will (or will not) enter the program. (p 27)

It has been found that two very different scoring systems can be used for these two purposes. Screening does not require the precision and accuracy of measurement called for in the important identification process.

Scoring for the purpose of screening (sorting students into those who may or may not be served by a gifted/talented program) can be served by an informal sorting system first reported for scoring a test by Horn and Smith (1945). Completed test booklets are scanned and simply sorted into *poor, average,* and *excellent* categories. The central *or average* group is then resorted into *weak, good,* and *very good* categories. Results of this two-step system are five stacks of test booklets in graded levels of competence (poor, weak, good, very good, and excellent). Screening decisions might include only *excellent* subjects or may include both *very good* and *excellent* subjects. The critical condition for determining a cut-off point would be how many people might best be served by a program and how many are needed for a pool of possible participants.

Identification scoring, requiring a more accurate and sensitive measurement, should be based upon the criteria scale and scoring system originally developed for Clark's Drawing Abilities Test. Inter-judge correlations for both of these scoring systems were high. An almost 100% agreement has been found in the sorting procedure among several sets of judges with varying degrees of experience with children's art work. In the research described here, a .90 inter-judge correlation was obtained among three judges on their use of the criteria scale and scoring procedure (the three judges were the author and two art education graduate students). This criteria-based system yields a specific, quantitative score for each subject; this makes it possible for subjects to be rank ordered. Critical identification decisions can then be made by selecting whatever percentage of high-scoring subjects are needed to fill available positions in a program.

It was noted earlier that scores on Clark's Drawing Abilities Test, or any other test, should not be used in isolation to accept or reject an applicant for a gifted/talented program in the visual arts. There are many reasons for this, and much has been written about the need to use several, very divergent criteria for identifying artistically talented students (Koppitz, 1968; Barron, 1972; Getzels and Csikszentmihalyi, 1976; Oregon State Department of Education, 1979; Stalker, 1981; Saunders, 1982; VanTassel-Baska, 1984; Clark and Zimmerman, 1984). Other criteria, such as intensity of desire to create art and/or to participate in a specialized program (Feldman, 1980; Clark and Zimmerman, 1984), aesthetic perception (Meier, 1942), perceptual skills (Grossman, 1970), sensitivity to visual phenomena (Goodman, 1977), cognitive complexity (Stalker, 1981), examination of a portfolio (Saunders, 1982), or nominations by self, parent, teacher, peer, or others qualified in the field (Oregon State Department of Education, 1979; Connecticut State Department of Education, 1980) have all been proposed as concomitant measures to be used with one another in various combinations.

I have often been asked to specify a cut-off score on Clark's Drawing Abilities Test that would segregate 'gifted' from 'nongifted' students; that is not possible because performance on the test will vary significantly from school to school or situation to situation. It is highly recommended that an arbitrary percentage of high scoring subjects appropriate to the needs of any local program be used; obviously, a relatively large percentage of high scorers would be chosen for a screening procedure and a smaller percentage would be chosen in an identification procedure.

The relationship noted among the four drawing tasks required by administration of Clark's Drawing Abilities Test is impressive (see Table 1). A high degree of inter item correlation among test items has not been reported for any of the earlier tests used in studies conducted from 1919 to the present (Clark, 1987).

This may help explain why few, if any, of these tests are used now to identify artistically gifted students for gifted/talented programs (Clark & Zimmerman, 1984).

Summary and Conclusions

High correlations between teachers' ratings in the Indiana University Summer Arts Institute and scores on this drawing test imply that the test predicts student performance in classes as divergent as drawing and painting, photography, ceramics, sculpture, print-making, computer graphics, and theater and dance. In other words, student performance on this series of four drawing tasks seems to predict performance in classes that may or *may not* require drawing skills. This is true because drawing well is as much an intellectual act as a physical or emotional one. Vinacke (1952) has noted that "no matter how original or valuable a creative conception, it cannot result in a work of art . . . unless its originator has the requisite skills to convert it into tangible form (p. 253). DiLeo (1973) has studied children's drawings as evidence of the mental and psychological state of his subjects and has claimed that "drawing is generally a valid expression of intelligence and as such correlates well with IQ tests" (p. 273). Few of the many people who have studied children's drawings in the past have focused their attention, or that of their readers, upon relationships among drawing abilities and previous learning, skill development, or general intelligence. There are still many unresolved questions about children's abilities in the visual arts. Who are the artistically gifted? What is their frequency of occurrence in the population? How do they learn and retain their abilities? What is the role of intelligence as a correlate? Clark's Drawing Abilities Test may help answer these and other questions as specific populations of artistically gifted students are served and are available as research subjects in gifted/talented programs throughout the country.

REFERENCES

Ahmad, P. S. (1982). The relationship of field-dependence-independence to subject matter and artistic style preferences of two-dimensional art works. Unpublished doctoral dissertation, Indiana University.

Barnes, E. (1893). A study on children's drawings. *Pedagogical Seminary*, 2(3), 455–463.

Barnes, E. (Ed.) (1902). *Studies in education*, Vol. 2. Philadelphia, PA: privately printed.

Barron, F. (1972). *Artists in the making*. New York: Seminar Press.

Broudy, H. S. (1972). *Enlightened cherishing: An essay on aesthetic education*. Urbana: University of Illinois Press.

Childs, H. G. (1915). Measurement of the drawing ability of two thousand one hundred and seventy seven children in Indiana city school systems by a supplemented Thorndike scale. *The Journal of Educational Psychology*, 6(7), 391–408.

Clark, A. B. (1897). The child's attitude toward perspective problems. In E. Barnes (Ed.). *Studies in education*, 1(18), 283–294.

Clark, G. A. (1982). In search of a concept of talent. In P. Godefrooij (Ed.). *INSEA preconference on research into ideology, learning, evaluation, and arts education: 1981 Congress book* (pp. 86–109). Rotterdam, the Netherlands: National Institute for Curriculum Development.

Clark, G. (1987). Chronology: Inquiry about children's drawing abilities and testing of art abilities. In G. Clark, E. Zimmerman, & M. Zurmuehlen. *Understanding art testing* (pp. 110–117). Reston. VA: National Art Education Association.

Clark, G., & Zimmerman, E. (1984). *Educating artistically talented students*, Syracuse, NY: Syracuse University Press.

Clark, G., Zimmerman, E., & Zurmuehlen, M. (1987). *Understanding art testing: Past influences, Norman C. Meier's contributions, present concerns, and future possibilities.* Reston, VA: National Art Education Association.

Connecticut State Department of Education. (1980). *Connecticut identification manual, Creative arts.* Hartford, CT: State Department of Education.

Cooke, E. (1885–1886). On art teaching and child nature. *Journal of Education, 8*(198), 12–15.

DiLeo, J. H. (1973). *Children's drawings as diagnostic aids.* New York: Brunner/Mazel.

DiLeo, J. H. (1977). *Child development: Analysis and synthesis.* New York: Brunner/Mazel.

Eisner, E. W. (1967). *The development of drawing characteristics of culturally advantaged and culturally disadvantaged children.* Project #3086. Washington, DC: Office of Education, Bureau of Research.

Eisner, E. W. (1972). *Educating artistic vision.* New York: Macmillan.

Feldhusen, J. F., Asher, J. W., & Hoover, S. M. (1984). Problems in the identification of giftedness, talent, or ability. *Gifted Child Quarterly, 28*(4), 149–151.

Feldman, D. H. (1980). *Beyond universals in cognitive development.* Norwood, NJ: Ablex.

Getzels, J. W., & Csikszentmihalyi, M. (1976). *The creative vision: A longitudinal study of problem finding in art.* New York: John Wiley and Sons.

Goodenough, F. (1924). The intellectual factor in children's drawings. Unpublished doctoral dissertation, Stanford University.

Goodenough, F. (1926). *Measurement of intelligence by drawings.* New York: Harcourt, Brace and World.

Goodman, E. (1977). The education of children gifted in the visual arts. *Trends In Education*, (Spring), 14–18.

Goodnow, J. (1977). *Children drawing.* Cambridge, MA: Harvard University Press.

Grossman, M. (1970). Perceptual style, creativity, and various drawing abilities. *Studies In Art Education, 11*(2), 51–54.

Gutteter, L. J. (1972). The relationship between the visual and haptic drawing styles and some psychological variables, age, sex, and previous art experience. *Studies in Art Education, 14*(1), 15–23.

Harris, D. B. (1963). *Children's drawings as measures of intellectual maturity: A revision and extension of Goodenough draw-a-man test.* New York: Harcourt, Brace and World.

Hildreth, G. (1941). *The child mind in evolution: A study of developmental sequences in drawing.* New York: Kings Crown Press.

Hollingworth, L. S. (1923). *Special talents and defects.* New York: Macmillan.

Horn, C. C. (1935). *The Horn art aptitude inventory.* Chicago, IL: C. H. Stoelting.

Horn, C., & Smith, L. F. (1945). The Horn art aptitude inventory. *Journal of Applied Psychology, 29*, 350–355.

Ivanoff, E. (1909). Researches experimentales sur le dessin des ecoliers de la Suisse romande: Correlation entre l'aptitude an dessin et les autres aptitudes

(Experimental research on the drawing of French speaking Swiss children: Correlation between drawing aptitude and other aptitudes). *Archives de Psychologie, 8,* 97–156.

Jones, E. E. (1922). The correlation of visual memory and perception with perspective with drawing ability. *School and Society, 15*(372) 174–176.

Karp, S. A., & Konstadt, N. I. (1963). *Children's embedded figures test.* New York: Cognitive Tests.

Kerschensteiner, I. G. (1905). Die Entwicklung der zeichnerischen Begabung (The development of drawing ability). Munich: Gerber.

Koppitz, E. M. (1968). *Psychological evaluation of children's human figure drawings.* New York: Grune &: Stratton.

Lark-Horovitz, B. (1941). On learning abilities in children recorded in a drawing experiment: 1. subject matter and 2. aesthetic and representational qualities. Journal of Experimental Education, *9*(4), 332–360.

Lewerenz, A. S. (1927). *Test of fundamental abilities in the visual arts.* Los Angeles: California Test Bureau.

Lewis, J. P. (1973). Spatial relations in children's drawings: A cross-generational comparison. *Studies in Art Education, 15*(3), 49–56.

Lovano-Kerr, J. (1983). Cognitive style revisited: Implications for research in art production and art criticism. *Studies In Art Education, 24*(3), 195–205.

Lowenfeld, V., & Brittain, W. L. (1984). *Creative and mental growth, 4th ed.* New York: Macmillan.

Manual, H. T. (1919). *Talent in drawing. An experimental study of the use of tests to discover special ability. School and Home Education Monograph #3.* Bloomington, IL: Public School Publishing Company.

Marland, S. P. (1972). *Education of the gifted and talented: Vol. 1. Report to the Congress of the United States by the U.S. Commissioner of Education.* Washington, DC: U.S. Government Printing Office.

McCarty, S. (1920). *Children's drawings.* Chicago, IL: Williams and Wilkins.

Meier, N. C. (1942). *Art in human affairs.* New York; McGraw-Hill.

Meumann. E. (1914). Die Analyse des Zeichnens und Modellierens (The analysis of drawing and modelling). *Vorlesungen zur Einfü*hrung in die experimentelle P*adagogik* (Lectures for an introduction to experimental pedagogy) (pp. 693–775). Leipsig: Englemann.

Munro, T., Lark-Horovitz, B., & Barnhardt, E. N. (1942). Children's art abilities: Studies at the Cleveland museum of art. *Journal of Experimental Education, 11* (2), 97–184.

National Assessment of Educational Progress (NAEP). (1977). *Design and drawing skills* (Art report #06-A-01). Washington, DC: U.S. Government Printing Office.

National Assessment of Educational Progress (NAEP). (1981). *Art and young Americans* (Art report #06-A-01). Denver. CO: Education Commission of the States.

Oliver, F. (1974). Le dessin enfantin, est-il une ecriture? (Is childish drawing handwriting?) Enfance, *3*(5), 183–216.

Oregon State Department of Education. (1979). *Identifying talented and gifted students.* Portland, OR: Northwest Regional Educational Laboratory.

Ricci, C. (1887). *L'Arte dei bambini* (The art of the child). Bologna (Italy): N. Zanchelli.

Rouma, G. (1913). *Le langage graphique de l'enfant* (The child's graphic language). Paris: Aecan.

Rouse, M. J. (1963). A comparison of Witkin's and Lowenfeld's theories of perceptual orientation. Unpublished doctoral dissertation, Stanford University.

Saunders, R. J. (1982). Screening and identifying the talented in art. *Roeper Review, 4*(3), 7–10.

Silver, R. (1983). *Silver drawing test of cognitive and creative skills.* Seattle, WA: Special Child Publications.

Silverman, R. H. (1982). *Learning about art: A practical approach.* Newport Beach, CA: Romar Arts.

Stalker, M. Z. (1981). Identification of the gifted in art. *Studies in Art Education, 22,* 49–56.

Swassing, R. H. (1985). *Teaching gifted children and adolescents.* Columbus, OH: Charles E. Merrill.

Thorndike, E. L. (1913). The measurement of achievement in drawing. *Teachers College Record, 14*(5), 1–39.

Thorndike, E. L. (1916). Tests of esthetic appreciation. *The Journal of Educational Psychology, 7*(10), 509–522.

Tiebout, C. (1933–1934). The psychophysical functions differentiating artistically superior from artistically inferior children. In H. S. Langfeld (Ed.). *Psychological monographs, 45* (pp. 108–133). Princeton, NJ: The Psychological Review Company.

Tiebout, C., & Meier, N. C. (1936). Artistic ability and general intelligence. *Psychological Monographs, 48*(1), 95–125.

Van Sommers, P. (1984). *Drawing and cognition: Descriptive and experimental studies of graphic production processes.* London: Cambridge University Press.

VanTassel-Baska, J. (1984). The talent search as an identification model. *Gifted Child Quarterly, 28*(4), 172–176.

Vernon, P. E., Adamson, G., & Vernon, D. (1972). *The psychology and education of gifted children.* Boulder, CO: Viewpoint Press.

Vinacke, W. E. (1952). *The psychology of thinking.* New York: McGraw-Hill.

Whipple, G. M. (1919). *Classes for gifted children.* Bloomington, IL: Public School Publishing Company.

Whitford, W. G. (1919a). Empirical study of pupil-ability in public-school art courses— Part 1. *The Elementary School Journal, 10*(1), 33–46.

Whitford, W. G. (1919b). Empirical study of pupil-ability in public-school art courses— Part II. *The Elementary School Journal, 10*(2), 95–105.

Wilson, B., Hurwitz, A., & Wilson, M. (1987). *Teaching drawing from art.* Worcester, MA: Davis Publications.

Wilson, B., and Wilson, M. (1977). An iconoclastic view of the imagery sources in the drawings of young people. *Art Education, 30*(1), 5–12.

Wilson, B., & Wilson, M. (1979). Figure structure, figure action, and framing in drawings by American and Egyptian children. *Studies in Art Education, 21*(1), 36–43.

Wilson, M., & Wilson, B. (1982). *Teaching children to draw: A guide for teachers and parents.* Englewood Cliffs, NJ: Prentice-Hall.

Youngblood, M. (1979). A non-verbal ability test. *Studies in Art Education 20*(3), 52–63.

Zimmerman, E. (1983). Cognitive style and related educational issues: New directions for research in art education. *Journal of Art and Design Education, 2*(1) 15–30.

12

The Characteristics Approach: Identification and Beyond

Sylvia Rimm

- Debbie was an "all A" student with an IQ score of 138. Motivated and conscientious, she wanted and needed more academic challenge than a typical student. She also thrived in the classroom, in extracurricular activities, and in the gifted/talented program. Responsible and independent, she has many excellent innovative ideas and displayed the leadership necessary to carry through plans and projects. Her parents both have a college education and their aspirations for their daughter were realistic, in that they and Debbie believed she would go on to college and probably to graduate school. She liked science and was leaning toward choosing a medical career. She had good friends and got along well with her family. Everyone who knew Debbie agreed that she was a truly gifted student.
- Amy was also an "all A" student, with an IQ score in the gifted range (131). She, too, was motivated and conscientious and fit into her school program well, in that she completed all assignments and some extra

Editor's Note: From Rimm, S. (1984). The characteristics approach: Identification and beyond. *Gifted Child Quarterly, 28*(4), 181–187. © 1984 National Association for Gifted Children. Reprinted with permission.

credit work. She participated in the gifted program and was pleased with her achievements. However, she really hated creative writing and individual, independent work. She always did her share when she worked with a peer group and could be counted on to be agreeable in group decision making. She learned information as quickly as Debbie but rarely contributed innovative ideas in class or among her peers. At home she was a model child, responsible and respectful. She expected to go on to college and since she really loved math and organizing figures, she thought she might become an accountant. However, she was equally good in verbal skills and hadn't yet ruled out other careers. Parents and teachers agreed that Amy's future looked bright.

- Dan was a C student whose IQ was in the superior range (128). He read mainly comic books and could recall baseball players' records over the past 25 years. His third-grade teacher had said his handwriting was too sloppy to read and his senior high English teacher said he couldn't express himself well enough to go to college. He never showed her his poetry and rarely volunteered in class. One could barely enter his bedroom because his hobbies, photographs, models, and tropical fish, as well as miscellaneous books, papers, and soiled clothes were strewn over all horizontal surfaces. He immersed himself in this ordered chaos for hours, contented, disturbing no one, oblivious to surrounding household activities. His mother said he was an average student and his dad described him as far below average. His mother thought he was unusual (positive) and his dad thought he was strange (not so positive). Neither had much confidence in his future career. He caused no real problems but seemed determined to direct his own life from early on. No one in his family or school ever considered him gifted.

Debbie's and Amy's parents and teachers were correct in predicting the future success of these girls. Debbie became a physician; Amy an accountant. Both found challenge and satisfaction in their careers. Debbie enjoyed the independence and creativity of research, as well as her personal and nurturant contact with patients. Amy felt comfortable in the organizational security of her numbers as well as the task specific components of her position. Their schools had served them well and had provided for their kinds of giftedness. They had *fit* within the school program.

Dan was much less predictable. His wide interests (often not school-related), his enthusiasm, his curiosity, and independence, which had not fit in elementary and secondary schools, served to direct him to the physics laboratory in college and graduate school. He became a prolific researcher and writer—no, not an Albert Einstein or a Nobel Prize winner, but the kind of creative scientist who helps to build the foundation for discovery and invention and contributes to making order out of chaos. He actually did learn to express himself in correct English and presented his research orally and in writing at research meetings and in journals. Dan managed to make his societal contributions despite, but not because of his elementary and secondary education. The "Dans" do not always achieve and create successfully; they are only rarely identified as gifted in our schools despite the fact that their behavioral characteristics are predictive of creativity. There have been numerous studies of typical traits, interests and activities of highly creative individuals in the arts and sciences (MacKinnon, 1978; Barron, 1969, 1978; Davis, Peterson, & Farley, 1973; Kagan, 1965; Schaefer, 1970; Davis, & O'Sullivan, 1980; Smith, 1966; Davis, 1975). Though researchers document this evidence regularly, schools have rarely used this information for the identification of or programming for gifted children.

In almost every G/T program in the country Debbie and Amy would have been identified. Dan would only have been nominated as gifted in programs where schools used a "characteristics approach" for identification. It was the recognition of this important gap in identification procedures that prompted the author to develop GIFT, *Gift Inventory for Finding Creative Talent*. It was her goal, literally, to *find* or discover among children in elementary schools those children who exhibit the behavioral characteristics which have typically been displayed by creative adults in their childhood. Although it was anticipated that some of these children would already be nominated as gifted by the usual IQ, achievement test, and teacher nomination criteria, it was also hypothesized that some students with high GIFT scores would exhibit poor academic performance, discipline problems, and creative behaviors which are not valued in the classroom.

PRINCIPLES FOR GUIDING IDENTIFICATION

What are the principles which should guide a school district in the identification of children as being gifted? What are the practical considerations in planning for screening for creativity? Considering the limitations of all kinds of testing, how can we combine objectivity with flexibility? Finally, how can we administer a screening efficiently so that it does not detract from the limited time and resources of a gifted program?

The identification process must match the goals of the particular gifted program. In the late 1950s gifted education was narrowly academically oriented. Fortunately, present programs almost always include creative and productive thinking explicitly defined as an important goal. If creativity is an objective of a gifted program, the identification component must surely include some measure of creativity. An identification procedure which does not include at least one reliable and valid measure of creativity is inadequate for a gifted program which includes creative thinking as a program goal.

A selection procedure must be objective enough to be considered fair by parents and teachers and flexible enough to compensate for the limitations of educational measurement. Teacher nomination is the most frequent source for the selection of creative students. Research documents the unreliability of teacher identification procedures (Rimm, 1976; Gallagher, 1966; Martinson, 1974). Although some teachers are adept at selecting creative students, many others are not attuned to creativity selection and mistakenly select only high achievers as being highly creative. Creativity in children exhibits itself in subtle ways. Although creativity tests and inventories are no more adequate for selection of creativity than are group IQ tests for selection of intelligence, they are more reliable and objective than the teacher selection procedure. Unless teachers are carefully educated as to the characteristics of highly creative children using teachers as the only selection measure is a mockery of creative identification. Furthermore, many teachers, particularly those in secondary schools, already feel overwhelmed by paperwork demands and justifiably resent completion of nomination checklists for the many students who enter their classrooms each day. Although teachers should be a part of selection, an objective measure must also be included. The combination will result in both objectivity and flexibility.

A test used for identification must meet the standards of valid educational measurement. It must be reliable and easy to administer to groups of students. Tests that require that teachers be trained for administration, or timed tests where small variations in time can significantly affect scores, are too burdensome for a school district to utilize. Unfortunately, they are frequently used without teacher training and this constitutes misuse. Tests should not take a long period of time for completion since educational time is valuable time.

Culture fairness or the indication that the test predicts validly for both minority and majority groups within a population is a consideration within most school districts. Cultural subgroups will vary among school districts, but the test should have been found valid for a population similar to the one for which it is being used.

Results from the test should be used for purposes beyond identification. A recent statement by Dr. Donald Treffinger summarizes this point succinctly. "Identification isn't worth anything unless it has an impact on programming" (1983). Scores should not be used as a single number for "cut-off" purposes, but should provide information which is useful for planning instruction and/or counseling for gifted students. Inasmuch as gifted programming should include a wide variety of services for gifted children, tests and inventory scores should be used for determining the needs of children selected for the program, as well as for facilitating the selection process.

RESEARCH BACKGROUND
OF GIFT, GIFFI, AND PRIDE

The creation of GIFT, GIFFI, and PRIDE and their research were guided by the principles explicitly stated in the foregoing section. A summary of each instrument and its validation will be presented briefly. For more detail, readers are advised to read past research papers (Rimm, 1982, 1983; Rimm & Davis, 1976, 1980; Rimm, Davis & Bien, 1982; Davis & Rimm, 1979, 1980).

Table 1   Sample Items for Dimensions of GIFT

Dimension	Item
Many Interests—High scorers are interested in art, writing, and learning about life long ago and in other countries. Low scorers have few interests and hobbies.	*Making up stories is a waste of time. Sometimes my mom or dad and I make things together. I like to learn about animals. I like to collect a lot of things. I like to read books about the future.
Independence—High scorers enjoy "aloneness." They prefer challenge and are not afraid to be different than their peers. Low scorers prefer being with others to being alone, give up on tasks easily, and are not likely to try new activities.	I have some really good ideas. I like things that are hard to do. *It's hard to find things to do when I'm alone. I like to try new things, even if I'm a little afraid. *I'm a lot like most of my friends.
Imagination—High scorers are curious, enjoy questioning, make believe and humor. Low scorers are more literal and realistic and less curious.	I like to take things apart to see how they work. *Real life stories are better than make-believe ones. *Playing make-believe games seems babyish. I like to make up jokes.

*Negatively scored.

Gift

Group Inventory for Finding Creative Talent was developed in 1975. It includes three forms for primary (K–2), elementary (3–4), and upper elementary (5–6) grades, respectively. GIFT items permit students to answer "yes" or "no" to statements reflecting their interests and attitudes. Although the original forms included 36 items each, in 1980 GIFT was revised and renormed to include 32, 34, and 33 items respectively for each level. A biographical component in which a father was part of a statement constituted the basis for eliminating items. Although these items had been validated in item analysis, it was kinder and more appropriate to omit these items since teachers indicated they had caused problems for children coming from nontraditional families.

Dimension scores for GIFT, derived by factor analysis, were introduced in 1982 and included Imagination, Independence, and Many Interests. Samples of items within each dimension are included in Table 1. GIFT is computer scored and returned to the school district within two weeks. An example of computer output is included in Table 2. Note that total scores are reported by percentile and Normal Curve Equivalent.[1] Dimension scores are reported by stanine.

Table 2   Facsimile of Computer Printout of GIFT Scores

The following are some important guidelines that need to be followed in using these scores: 1) High scores (85–99 percentile) indicate that the child has characteristics similar to those which are typical of highly creative children. Characteristics measured by this inventory include interest range, independence, perseverance, flexibility, curiosity, and biographical information. 2) Low or average scores do not indicate that a child is necessarily not creative. The inventory was not designed to screen children out of gifted programs.

	Anytown, USA			George Washington School		
Grade 5		Instrument Level: GIFT Upper Elementary Level				
	Test Date 10/1/83			Teacher: Mrs. Carlson		
Name	Many Interests	Independence	Imagination	Total Score	%ile	NCE[2]
	Stanine[1]	Stanine	Stanine			
1. Sara	9	9	7	32	99	99
2. Don	5	4	2	17	17	30
3. Diana	7	5	6	24	71	61.8
4. Jeremy	9	5	9	28	94	81.9
5. Kirsten	5	7	7	25	79	66.6
6. John	9	7	9	30	98	92
Mean	7.333	6.167	6.667	26.00		71.88
Standard Deviation	1.966	1.835	2.582	5.33		25.00

Description of Dimensions

1. Many Interests—High scorers are interested in art, writing, learning about life long ago and in other countries, and enjoy many hobbies. Low scorers have few interests and hobbies.

2. Independence—High scorers enjoy "aloneness." They prefer challenge and are not afraid to be different than their peers. Low scorers prefer being with others to being alone, give up on tasks easily, and are not likely to try new activities.

3. Imagination—High scorers are curious, enjoy questioning, make believe, and humor. Low scorers are more literal and realistic and less curious.

Explanation of Scores

[1]Stanine—Standard score with a mean of 5 and a standard deviation of 2.

[2]NCE (Normal Curve Equivalent)—Normalized standard score with a mean of 50 and a standard of 21.06.

GIFFI I and GIFFI II

Group Inventory For Finding Interests, was designed for the middle/junior high school level, grades 6–9. GIFFI II was created for high school students in grades 9–12. GIFFI I and GIFFI II include 60 items. They use a five-point rating scale; "No," "To a small extent," "Average," "More than average," and "Definitely." The GIFFI Inventories have been factor analyzed and arranged into five dimensions including Creative Arts and Writing, Challenge-Inventiveness, Confidence, Imagination, and Many Interests. These dimensions with their sample items are included in Tables 3 and 4.

Table 3   Sample Items for Dimensions of GIFFI I

Dimension	Item
Creative Arts and Writing—High scorers enjoy creative art, stories, poetry, and music. Low scorers do not enjoy active involvement in the arts.	I like to make up my own songs. *Making up stories is a waste of time. I like to do handicraft projects. I have thought about a job as an artist or a writer.
Challenge-Inventiveness—High scorers are risk-takers. They enjoy difficult tasks and inventing and thinking of new ideas. Low scorers tend not to persevere and prefer easier tasks with less risk.	I like things that are hard to do. I like to invent things. *I try to stay away from things that are very difficult. I can work on a hobby for a long time and not get bored.
Confidence—High scorers find school easy and believe they have good ideas. They are more independent of peer pressure and willing to try new opportunities. Low scorers have a poorer self-image and find it important to be like their peers.	I have a good sense of humor. It's all right to sometimes change the rules of a game. *I am a lot like most of my friends. *It's important to me to participate in team sports.
Imagination—High scorers are curious, enjoy questioning, "aloneness," and travel. They like new and imaginary ideas. Low scorers are more literal and realistic and less curious.	I like to take a walk alone. *Playing make-believe games seems babyish. I used to have (or still have) a pretend playmate. I think using your imagination is important.
Many Interests—High scorers have many hobbies and are interested in drama, literature, life in other countries, the past, the future, and many other topics. Low scorers have fewer interests and hobbies.	I am interested in a lot of different things. I often think about what is right and what is wrong. I have taken art, dancing or music lessons outside of school because I wanted to. I have had collections of unusual objects.

*Negatively scored.

Pride

*PR*eschool *I*nterest *DE*scriptor was developed in response to requests by school districts for a preschool and kindergarten screening instrument. Since GIFT had inadequate reliability at the kindergarten level, PRIDE was created as a parent report inventory. It was based on the research of creative characteristics of preschool and kindergarten children and has 50 items with response options similar to those used for GIFFI. Preliminary factor analysis provides dimension scores for PRIDE including Many Interests, Independence-Perseverance, Imagination-Playfulness, and Originality. Table 5 includes sample items of PRIDE arranged by dimension. Although PRIDE is presently in preliminary publication, further research will be conducted to expand the norm group and concurrent validation.

Table 4   Sample Items for Dimensions of GIFFI II

Dimension	Item
Creative Arts and Writing—High scorers enjoy creative art, stories, poetry, and music. Low scorers do not enjoy active involvement in the arts.	I am very artistic. I try to use metaphors and analogies in writing. When I was a child, I remember creating games, stories, poems or art work more than other children did. I have considered a career as an artist or writer.
Challenge-Inventiveness—High scorers are risk-takers. They enjoy difficult tasks and inventing and thinking of new ideas. Low scorers tend not to persevere and prefer easier tasks with less risk.	I enjoy trying new approaches to problems. I am a risk-taker. I am able to work intensely on a project for many hours. I would enjoy a job with unforeseeable difficulties.
Confidence—High scorers consider themselves to have good intellectual and creative ability. They consider themselves to be inventive and witty. Low scorers do not believe they are imaginative, creative, or intellectually able.	I am quite original and imaginative. I am often inventive or ingenious. I would rate myself high in "intuition" or "insightfulness." I often become totally engrossed in a new idea.
Imagination—High scorers are curious, enjoy questioning, "aloneness," and travel. They like new and imaginary ideas. Low scorers are more literal and realistic and less curious.	I would like to explore new cities alone, even if I get lost. I often think like a child. I am unconventional in many ways. My ideas are often considered "impractical" or even "wild."
Many Interests—High scorers have many hobbies and are interested in drama, literature, life in other countries, the past, the future, and many other topics. Low scorers have fewer interests and hobbies.	Some of my past or present hobbies would be considered "unusual." I have a great many interests. I read over 20 books a year. I have performed music with school or community groups.

Reliability has been established for all inventories. The Spearman-Brown formula for the split-half method was used for calculating correlation coefficients for GIFT and *they were* .80, .86 and .88 for the primary, elementary, and upper elementary forms, respectively. Reliability coefficients for kindergarten were not acceptably high. Internal reliability coefficients for GIFFI I ranged between .88 and .91. For GIFFI II, they ranged between .85 and .96. For PRIDE, the internal reliability coefficient was .92. As one would expect, for the most part, reliability increases as respondents increase in age. Very young children answer self-report inventories less reliably than teenagers or adults.

The content validity of GIFT, GIFFI I, and GIFFI II were established by including items which assessed personality and biographical characteristics of creative persons as described by authors of other creativity instruments. Instruments researched include: the Getzels and Jackson (1962) creativity tests; the Torrance Tests of Creative Thinking (Torrance, 1966); the Pennsylvania Assessment of Creative Tendency (Rookey, 1974); creativity scales for the Adjective Checklist (Smith & Schaefer, 1969; Domino, 1970); and How Do You Think? (Davis, 1975). The main characteristics included in GIFT and GIFFI are curiosity, independence, flexibility, perseverance, and variety of interests. Content validity of PRIDE was established based on the research of characteristics of preschool and kindergarten children as reported in papers by Auerbach (1972), Newland (1976), Johnson (1978), Fuqua, Bartsch, and Phye (1975) and Torrance (1965).

Concurrent validity studies in which GIFT, GIFFI, and PRIDE scores were correlated with outside measures of creativity have now been conducted among varied subpopulations in this country as well as in other countries. Almost regardless of population makeup, validity correlation coefficients have been moderate but statistically significant. There have been a few exceptions and these have been reported in previous publications. The criterion related validity studies used mainly the same outside criteria. For GIFT, the main validity criterion was a composite score consisting of teacher ratings of student creativeness and experimenter ratings of short stories and pictures. The three criteria each involved a 1–5 rating scale so that scores could be combined and equally weighted before calculating validity correlations with the inventory. The teacher rating was based on a 1 to 5 scale where "5" was described as "highly creative, has many and original ideas related to art, music, class materials, or out-of-class interests," and "1" was described as "very low creativity level, has rarely expressed any creative ideas in any verbal musical, or artistic form."

The validity criterion was modified for GIFFI I and GIFFI II, since with junior and senior high school students, the drawing (art) criterion was found not to discriminate among more and less creative students. In all of the present GIFFI validation studies, then, the two criteria were: (a) teacher ratings of the creativeness of each student on a five-point scale, and (b) ratings of the creativeness of students' short stories by trained raters. These were then combined into a single validating criterion.

The criterion for concurrent validity used for PRIDE included teacher ratings of creativity, a drawing and a dictated brief story about the drawing. Raters familiarized themselves with developmental stages of children's art (Gardner, 1980) in order to recognize the typical differences in the growth of artistic expression exhibited by young children.

GIFT was found to be valid using the specified three outside criteria for the following separate groups of children: U.S.—rural, suburban, urban White, urban Black, urban Hispanic, rural Native American, learning disability, and gifted program students; International—French suburban, Israeli mixed population, Israeli culturally deprived, Israeli gifted, Christian, Moslem and Druse

Table 5   Sample Items for Dimensions of PRIDE

Dimension	Items
Many Interests—High scorers are curious and ask questions. They show high interest in learning, stories, books, and things around them. Low scorers show less curiosity and have fewer interests.	My child seems to like to think about ideas. My child likes to take things apart to see how they work. My child gets very interested in things around her/him. My child likes to try new things.
Independence-Perseverance—High scorers play alone and do things independently. They do not give up easily and persevere even with difficult tasks. Low scorers tend to prefer easier tasks and are more likely to follow the lead of other children.	My child gets interested in things for a long time. *My child gets bored easily. *My child usually does whatever other children do. My child likes to pick his/her own clothes to wear to school.
Imagination-Playfulness—High scorers enjoy make-believe, humor, and playfulness. Low scorers tend to be more serious and realistic.	My child spends much time playing make-believe. My child and I make jokes together. My child likes to play out in the rain. My child often says things that are funny.
Originality—High scorers tend to have unusual ideas and ask unusual questions. They are inventive in their art and play and tend to think differently than other children. Low scorer's ideas and art work appear to be more typical of children of similar age.	My child asks unusual questions. My child has unusual ideas. My child seems to do things differently than other children. My child often points to unusual things around her/him.

*Negatively scored.

Arabic populations, Australian lower and middle class urban populations, an urban population in Taiwan, Australian lower and middle class rural populations, and a Spanish (Spain) urban population.

GIFFI I and GIFFI II have now been validated for several U.S. mixed racial populations including urban, suburban, and rural communities in Wisconsin, Texas, Illinois, and New York state as well as in Australia.

PRIDE's validation has been limited to Wisconsin and New York State but research is *continuing for PRIDE* as well as for GIFT, GIFFI I, and GIFFI II.

USING CREATIVITY INVENTORIES FOR SCREENING

There are ideal ways to use creativity inventories as part of screening for gifted programming and there are some minimal ways. Conversely, there are also some ways which are inappropriate and dangerous. We can begin with the way *not* to use GIFT, GIFFI, and PRIDE. *Do not use cut-off scores for screening gifted children out of programs.* This statement is made in all inventory technical manuals as well as on the computer output. The primitive level of the science of measurement, as well as the subtlety of creative potential, should prohibit such misuse of any creativity measure. Do use the total score and the dimension scores to plan for the creative needs of already identified gifted children. Do use the total score and the dimension scores to help find children who have creative characteristics and who are not already identified for the gifted program.

Minimally, children who have been identified as academically gifted should have the opportunity to complete a GIFT or GIFFI self-report. It will provide teachers, coordinators, and counselors with a shorthand form of information about the child's behavioral characteristics which relate to creativity. A brief example of use for the high IQ, high academic achiever who scores low on independence follows: The child will need guidance and teacher support to help develop independence. The discussion of conformity and peer pressure certainly needs to be part of his/her gifted programming. If teachers select an appropriate peer group for such discussion, it should include high independence students in order that peers can communicate the critical value of independence. Peer conformity is the antithesis of creativity and should be explored and not labeled as good social adjustment for gifted children.

Ideally, a screening instrument should be used for all children. It need not be used each year, but, for example, if a creativity inventory was administered at every other grade level, all children could complete a self-report every other year. Administration time is brief. Instructions are simple and reliable. Timing is not an issue or a problem. Teachers may read the items to children at lower grade levels to avoid missing children who are poor readers. Broad screening will result in discovering children with high interest, imagination, and independence which is not being expressed in school achievement. Gifted programming can then determine how counseling and curriculum can help these children to focus their high creativity positively. If society claims to value creativity, then gifted programming must go beyond providing academic challenge. Schools must combine our understanding of creative process, creative attitudes, and creative characteristics with the acquisition of information synergistically so that gifted programming can complement the acquisition of knowledge with creative thinking.

Jeff's teachers sat around the conference table puzzling about this eighth-grade boy. He had been labeled learning disabled, yet no one was quite sure about him. His WISC-R test score was 121 and there was considerable scatter among his separate scores. Some were very high; others were below average.

Excerpts from teacher discussion sounded like this:

"Do you suppose I should grade him on a pass/fail criterion since he's learning disabled?"

"I'd like to drop him out of band. He's disruptive and prevents other students from learning."

"He's doing a fine job in math. I don't see any real problem."

"I know he tested as a poor reader, but today he got a perfect score on a Reading Comprehension test. I thought he might have cheated so I asked him to take the test again. I was angry and he was angry, but he got a perfect score again."

"My concern in social studies is that he doesn't get his homework in. He tells me unusual stories of why he hasn't done it and I don't know whether to believe him or not. He seems sincere and his excuses are imaginative, but he doesn't perform."

His grades are poor. His homework is sporadic. We don't know if he's bright or slow and we're not even sure when he's telling the truth. What do we do with Jeff? He's been labeled LD, a behavior problem, a manipulative child, a lazy careless student, and a storyteller. He doesn't *fit* in this school program.

Jeff's GIFFI score is 98th percentile. Can gifted identification find the Jeffs? Can gifted programming find the Dan who was described earlier in this paper? Can we use self-report inventories to help us identify children with character-istics of high creativity? And then can we move beyond identification, to pro-viding the focus and support for the creative children who don't presently fit in our G/T programs or in our schools?

NOTE

1. Normal Curve Equivalents are normalized standard scores with a mean of 50 and a standard deviation of 21.06.

REFERENCES

Auerbach, A. G. The biociative or creative act in the nursery school. *Young Children*, 1972 (October).

Barron, F. *Creative person and creative process*. NYC: Holt, 1969.

Barron, F. An eye more fantastical. In G. S. Davis, & J. A. Scott (Eds.), *Training creative thinking*. Huntington, NY: Krieger, 1978.

Davis, G. A. In frumious pursuit of the creative person. *Journal of Creative Behavior*, 1975, 9, 75–87.

Davis, G. A., & O'Sullivan, M. Taxonomy of creative objectives: The model AUTA. *Journal of Creative Behavior*, 1980, 14(3), 149–160.

Davis, G. A., Peterson, J. A., & Farley, F. H. Attitudes, motivation, sensation seeking, and belief in ESP as predictors of real creative behavior. *Journal of Creative Behavior*, 1973, 7, 31–39.

Davis, G. A., & Rimm, S. Identification and counseling of the creatively gifted. In N. Colangelo & R. T. Zaffrann (Eds.), *New voices in counseling the gifted*. Dubuque, IA: Kendall/Hunt, 1979.

Davis, G. A., & Rimm, S. *GIFFI II: Group inventory for finding interests.* Watertown, WI: Educational Assessment Service, 1980.

Domino, G. Identification of potentially creative persons from the Adjective Check List. *Journal of Consulting and Clinical Psychology,* 1970, *35,* 48–51.

Fuqua, R. W., Bartsch, T. W., & Phye, G. D. An investigation of the relationship between cognitive tempo and creativity in preschool age children. *Child Development,* 1975, *46,* 779–782.

Gallagher, J. J. *Research summary on gifted education.* Springield, IL: State Department of Public Instruction, 1966.

Gardner, H. *Artful scribbles, the significance of children's drawings.* NYC: Basic Books, 1980.

Getzels, J. W., & Jackson, P. W. *Creativity and intelligence.* NYC: Wiley, 1962.

Johnson, J. E. Mother-child interaction and imaginative behavior of preschool children. *Journal of Psychology,* 1978, *100,* 123–129.

Kagan, J. Impulsive and reflective children: Significance of conceptual tempo. In J. D. Krumboltz (Ed.), *Learning and the educational process.* Chicago: Rand McNally, 1965.

MacKinnon, D. W. Educating for creativity: A modern myth? In G.A. Davis & J. A. Scott (Eds.), *Training creative thinking.* Huntington, NY: Krieger, 1978.

Martinson, R. A. *The identification of the gifted and talented.* Ventura, CA: Office of the Ventura Superintendent of Schools, 1974.

Newland, T. E. *The gifted in socioeducational perspective.* Englewood Cliffs, NJ: Prentice Hall, 1976.

Rimm, S. *GIFT: Group inventory for finding creative talent.* Watertown, WI: Educational Assessment Service, 1976.

Rimm, S. *PRIDE: Preschool interest descriptor.* Watertown, WI: Educational Assessment Service, Inc., 1982.

Rimm, S. Identifying creativity, Part 1. *G/C/T,* 1983 (March/April), 34–37.

Rimm, S., & Davis, G. A. GIFT: An instrument for the identification of creativity. *Journal of Creative Behavior,* 1976, *10*(3), 178–182.

Rimm, S., & Davis, G. A. *GIFFI I: Group inventory for finding interests.* Watertown, WI: Educational Assessment Service, 1980.

Rimm, S., Davis, G. A., & Bien, Y. Identifying creativity: A characteristics approach. *Gifted Child Quarterly,* 1982 (Fall), *26*(4), 165–171.

Rookey, T. J. Validation of a creativity test, the 100 students study. *Journal of Creative Behavior,* 1974, *8,* 211–213.

Schaefer, C. E. *Biographical inventory-creativity.* San Diego, CA: Educational and Industrial Testing Services, 1970.

Smith, J. M. *Setting conditions for creative teaching in the elementary school.* Boston: Allyn & Bacon, 1966.

Smith, J. M., & Schaefer, C. E. Development of a creativity scale for the adjective check-list. *Psychological Reports,* 1969, *25,* 87–92.

Torrance, E. P. *Gifted children in the classroom.* NYC: Macmillan, 1965.

Torrance, E. P. *Torrance tests of creative thinking.* Bensenville, IL: Scholastic Testing Service, 1966.

Treffinger, D. Blending gifted education with the total school program. Wisconsin Council for Gifted and Talented state meeting, Wausau, WI, October, 1983.

13

The Influence of Identification Practices, Race and SES on the Identification of Gifted Students

Jamieson A. McKenzie

Princeton Regional Schools

Identification procedures for gifted programs reinforce social inequalities while missing some of our most promising students. This study reports a survey of 461 (82.5%) New Jersey school districts. The results show that there are significant relationships between G/T participation rates and 1) race, 2) spending per pupil, 3) property, value per pupil, and 4) the socioeconomic status of school districts. The study also found excessive reliance on standardized tests. The author calls for a broadened, developmental definition of giftedness.

Editor's Note: From McKenzie, J. A. (1986). The influence of identification practices, race and SES on the identification of gifted students. *Gifted Child Quarterly, 30*(2), 93–95. © 1986 National Association for Gifted Children. Reprinted with permission.

Two main problems arise with regard to the use of standardized achievement tests and intelligence scales in identifying gifted and talented children for special educational programs. The first is that these tests may reflect racial and/or socioeconomic bias and reinforce existing inequalities in selection of these children for special programs (Bailey & Harbin, 1980). The second problem is that these tests may fail to measure some traits, behaviors and potentials that are significant indicators of giftedness and thereby fail to identify some of our most promising or potentially capable students. Renzulli (1981) argues that many of the world's greatest talents would not be identified to participate in gifted programs if one were to rely solely upon IQ scores. Bernal (1981) advocates "inclusionism"—an approach which identifies any child who demonstrates giftedness *prima facie* or gifted potential on one or more indicators of the trait under consideration. Jenkins-Friedman (1982) warns of the "cosmetic" use of multiple selection criteria which mask the reality that standardized test scores still control original screening.

A fundamental question underlying the issues discussed above is the meaning of "giftedness," a hitherto unresolved debate. Those who equate giftedness with genetic endowment may focus their attention on the development of accurate measures of native ability. Those who believe that gifts may be nurtured, expanded and cultivated may call for identification procedures which allow a variety of children to qualify, not just those who perform well on standardized tests, classroom tasks, or academic challenges. Reis and Renzulli (1982) call for a broadened conception of giftedness which enables 15–25% of the school population to be served by the program. Likewise, Feldman (1979) takes the position that "All children are gifted and the purpose of education is to promote excellence in as many forms as possible" (pp. 662–663). Yarborough and Johnson (1983) conclude that there is a gap between theory and practice. Their survey showed that despite an avowed intent to "find" potential giftedness, most identification procedures fail to live up to expectations. A national survey of identification practices by Alvino, McDonnel, and Richert (1981) also found heavy reliance upon achievement and IQ tests. They concluded that " . . . many tests/instruments are being used for purposes and populations completely antithetical to those for which they were intended" (p. 129). Renzulli, Reis, and Smith (1981) also urge that consideration be given to task commitment and creativity in identifying gifted students.

Little research has been devoted to the evaluation of identification procedures in minority and/or disadvantaged student populations. This article reports the findings of a survey of gifted/talented programs in New Jersey which examined whether these programs tend to reflect and reinforce existing patterns of inequality in the identification of gifted youth. The study sought to determine if G/T programs are more likely to serve the wealthy, the white and those from high status socioeconomic backgrounds than the poor, the disadvantaged, the minorities and those from low status socioeconomic backgrounds.

DESIGN OF THE STUDY

The primary method used to identify the practices that characterize gifted education programs in New Jersey was a survey of all school districts other than special education and vocational schools. A total of 461 (82.5%) of 559 school districts responded to the survey. Data with regard to socioeconomic factors, property value, and per pupil spending were obtained from State Department of Education records, and data with regard to racial participation in 80 of the state's districts were obtained from the United States Department of Civil Rights Fall 1982 Survey (the school-by-school forms are on file with the Department of Civil Rights). Chi square tests were used to test differences between frequencies. All tests yielded chi squares which were significant beyond the .01 level of significance.

FINDINGS

A. Racial Data

Data compiled from the Civil Rights Survey of 1982 showed that the representation of different racial/ethnic groups in G/T programs surveyed in New Jersey is disproportionate to their share of the overall population. While Asians represent only 3.55% of the total gifted population (18,584), their incidence of G/T participation (Asians in G/T program/Total Asian population) is 10.11%. Whites had the second highest incidence of participation (6.85%) followed by native Americans (3.85%), blacks (2.42%), and hispanics (1.87%). These differences were statistically significant (chi square = 5148, 4df). The percentages of the total G/T population for whites, native Americans, blacks and hispanics were 72.64%, .06%, 17.25%, and 6.50% respectively.

B. Identification Data

The three identification practices cited most frequently are Teacher Nominations (90.0%), Achievement Tests (89.6%), and IQ Tests (82.0%). "Culture Free Tests" were least frequently cited with only 16 districts mentioning their use, and the statistics are as follows: Teacher Nomination - 90%; Achievement Tests - 89.6%; IQ Tests - 82%; Grades - 56.4%; Parent Nominations - 54.7%; Informal Ratings - 33%; Peer Nominations - 27.8%; Creativity Tests - 26.5%; Self Nomination - 24.7%; Appeal - 20%; Interview - 17.1%; Audition - 9.1%; Community Nomination - 8.7%; and Culture Free Tests - 3.5%.

Even though considerable disagreement exists over the feasibility of creating a genuinely "culture free test," it is significant that few districts claimed the use of such tests. The tests cited echoed the findings of Alvino, McDonnel, and Richert (1981) who also found few tests that claimed to be culture-free being used.

C. Socioeconomic Data

The New Jersey Department of Education groups school districts into categories which reflect socioeconomic level based on information from the U.S. Census report. These are called DFG groups (District Factor Groups). The groups ascend in affluence, education and socioeconomic status from Group A, which is primarily urban and poor, up to Group J, which is primarily suburban and wealthy. There is a statistically significant relationship (chi square = 6472, 10 df) between DFG group and level of G/T participation as shown below. Participation climbs from 4.4% in Group A to 13.8% and 12.1% in Groups I and J.

DFG Group	% Students in G/T Program	Number of Students
A	4.4	5,921
B	8.1	1,953
C	8.8	2,210
D	9.0	3,840.
E	13.6	6,328
F	9.9	4,172
G	8.3	4,084
H	9.8	5,226
I	13.8	5,059
J	12.1	5,233

A statistically significant relationship was found (chi square = 2.55, 4 df) for spending per pupil and the percentage of G/T participation in a school district, with districts spending less than $3,000 at 8.1% and less than $4,500 at 8.5%, while participation climbs to 12.7% and 12.3% at the next two levels of spending. Districts spending more than $4,500 drop dramatically back down to 6.5%. Students in more affluent districts have a higher likelihood of participation in a gifted program.

A statistically significant relationship also existed between property value per student and G/T participation in a district (chi square = 2509, 3df) once again demonstrating that students in more affluent districts have a greater likelihood of participating in a gifted program. The percentage of participation rises from 6.6% for assessed property value less than $100,000 per student, to 10.7% for assessed value from $100,000–$200,000 per student, to a high of 12.1% for assessed value more than $200,000 per pupil.

DISCUSSION

There are vast disparities in the resources available to different school districts in New Jersey for the education of children. While these disparities are meant to be offset by state aid, actual spending per pupil still varies dramatically from district to district, and this study has shown that the provision of gifted and talented programs varies dramatically from district to district. It is doubtful that equality of educational opportunity can exist when the funding of educational programs relies so heavily upon local resources that inequalities between communities are translated into inequalities in educational programs. Reform of school finance is an essential first step if schooling is to be provided in a democratic and just manner.

A second major concern raised by the data in this study is the tendency for districts to operationalize definitions of giftedness which work to the advantage of the already advantaged. These definitions lead to identification procedures which spotlight those children whose gifts are most readily apparent. These procedures in turn skew the provision of services to those who already demonstrate ability, often on tasks which are easier for those with socially and economically advantaged backgrounds. As a result of this approach to giftedness, the inequities flowing from inequalities between communities are further exaggerated. Minorities and the disadvantaged have far less chance of participating in G/T programs than do advantaged members of the majority culture. Those with a headstart in the race are effectively separated from those who were handicapped by reason of social conditions.

We must turn to a definition of giftedness which will stress the importance of *development*. Gifted programs should be viewed as an investment in human potential, and identification procedures should be based upon a broadened and more flexible conception of giftedness which places greater emphasis upon the discovery, development and nurturing of hitherto undiscovered gifts.

CONCLUSION

It is time to bring theory and practice back into congruence. The work of Reis and Renzulli (1982), Taylor and Ellison (1983), Meeker and Meeker (1976) and many others offer hope that identification procedures can be modified to correct the patterns identified by this study, but much remains to be done in order to bridge the "theory-practice" gap reported by Yarborough and Johnson (1983), Alvino, McDonnel, and Richert (1981), and this study.

REFERENCES

Alvino, J., McDonnel, R., & Richert, S. (1981). National survey of identification practices in gifted and talented education. *Exceptional Children, 48,* 124–132.

Bailey, D., & Harbin, G. (1980). Nondiscriminatory evaluation. *Exceptional Children, 46,* 590–596.

Bernal, E. (1981). Special problems and procedures for identifying minority gifted students. Paper presented at the Council for Exceptional Children Conference on the Exceptional Bilingual Child, New Orleans, February, 1981.

Feldman, D. (1979). Toward a nonelitist conception of giftedness. *Phi Delta Kappan, 60,* 660–663.

Jenkins-Friedman, R. (1982). Myth: Cosmetic use of multiple selection criteria. *Gifted Child Quarterly, 26,* 24–26.

Meeker, M., & Meeker, R. (1976). *Structure of intellect learning abilities test.* El Segundo, CA: SOI Institute.

Reis, S., & Renzulli, J. (1982). The case for a broadened conception of giftedness. *Phi Delta Kappan, 63,* 619–620.

Renzulli, J. (1981). Myth: The gifted constitute 3–5% of the population (Dear Mr. and Mrs. Copernicus: We regret to inform you . . .). *Gifted Child Quarterly, 26,* 11–14.

Renzulli, J., Reis, S., & Smith, L. (1981). *The revolving door identification model.* Mansfield Center, CT: Creative Learning Press.

Taylor, C., & Ellison, R. (1983). Searching for student talent resources relevant to all USDE types of giftedness. *Gifted Child Quarterly, 27,* 99–106.

Yarborough, B., & Johnson, R. (1983). Identifying the gifted: A theory practice gap. *Gifted Child Quarterly, 27,* 135–138.

14

Labeling Gifted Youngsters: Long-Term Impact on Families

Nicholas Colangelo

Penny Brower

The University of Iowa

This study examined the long-term effects of the "gifted" label on the family system. The families in this study had at least one child identified as gifted a minimum of five years prior to the study. The results of the study show that the long-term effects of the gifted label are in part a reverse of the reported immediate effects. Research on immediate effects indicates difficulties for non-labeled siblings. Long-term effects indicate that siblings "came to terms" with the label and did not seem to harbor negative feelings or recollections. While the families reported an overall positive attitude toward the gifted member, it was the gifted member who seemed less certain of the positive feelings of siblings and parents regarding the label.

Editor's Note: From Colangelo, N., & Brower, P. (1987). Labeling gifted youngsters: Long-term impact on families. *Gifted Child Quarterly*, *31*(2), 75-78. © 1987 National Association for Gifted Children. Reprinted with permission.

INTRODUCTION

A report from the U.S. Commissioner of Education Sidney P. Marland (1972), addressing the status of education of gifted and talented children concluded that both the process of identification and the provision of special programs for the gifted were critically inadequate. Congress responded by "implementing a Federal role in education of gifted and talented individuals." The definition of "gifted and talented" used to guide the implementation of Federal programs is as follows:

> Gifted and talented children are those identified by professional quali-
> fied persons who by virtue of outstanding abilities, are capable of high
> performance. These are children who require differentiated educational
> programs and/or services beyond those normally provided by the reg-
> ular school program in order to realize their contribution to self and
> society. (p. 2)

This definition indicated that deficits in the process of identification of the gifted and the supply of programs designed to stimulate the development of this newly "discovered" natural resource were to be systematically amelio-rated. This Congressional action stimulated research into the identification and education of the gifted, as well as the development of new programs for the gifted.

Within the report from the Commissioner of Education it was acknowl-edged that the concept of special programming was somewhat alien to "egali-tarian" school systems. Identification of the gifted was made a priority with minimal consideration given to the social and psychological costs and benefits for those ultimately identified and their families.

Hobbs (1975) articulated the central dilemma associated with the labeling of children. He observed that the classification of school learning difficulties, whether based on cognitive or emotional factors, is a practical necessity in order to provide appropriate special programs for youngsters who cannot learn in regular classrooms. The problem with labeling is that a student becomes iden-tified with the learning difficulty. Stereotypic attitudes and beliefs associated with the label can be falsely attributed to each labeled student. This, in turn, shapes the way others interact with the student and influences that student's self-perceptions. The adverse effects of labels on special education students have been widely acknowledged (Jones, 1972; Rist & Harrell, 1982). The effects of labeling a youngster "gifted" (typically viewed as a positive label) become even more problematic. Here we have youngsters who are labeled because they deviate from the norm in a positive way, i.e., they are considerably "above normal" in intelligence or creativity. However, their positive qualities do not assure acceptance or appreciation (Robinson, 1986). American society in general and schools in particular are ambivalent toward gifted. They are both admired and envied, and mistrusted (Colangelo & Dettman, 1985; Weiss & Gallagher, 1980).

Labeling: Effects on Families

Unfortunately, the issue of the effects of the gifted label on family dynamics has generated little empirical research. Peterson (1977) found that the presence of a gifted child in the family was associated with increased competition in the family and sibling jealousy. Colangelo and Kelly (1983), Fisher (1981), Hackney (1981) and Sunderlin (1981) also reported on the negative impact of the gifted label on family dynamics and adjustment difficulties among siblings. Albert (1980), in a major longitudinal study, showed that the gifted child receives a special position in the family and that family attention and resources are channeled to this youngster in greater proportion and intensity than to other siblings.

Cornell (1983) reported a research study that will probably spur further research. In the *American Journal of Orthopsychiatry*, Cornell reported on his study to assess the impact of the label "gifted child" on the child, parents, and siblings. He found that the label enhances the child's status in the family and affects the parents' perceptions of the child. The perception of parents is mixed in that both parents don't always agree on the accuracy of the label. When both parents agree that the child is gifted, they have a positive reaction to the child. When one parent disagrees with the label the reaction toward the child is mixed and usually more negative. When both parents disagree with the gifted label, the label is typically not perceived in a positive light.

The most interesting and potentially important finding in Cornell's research was the evidence that siblings of gifted students were significantly less adjusted emotionally and socially than siblings of nongifted students. Siblings of gifted students have received minimal research attention in gifted education.

Purpose of the Study

While the effects of labeling a youngster "gifted" have not been widely and systematically studied, the few studies reported do indicate a cautious and mixed reaction. The label has strong effects on family dynamics and in particular there seems to be some evidence that the label has negative impact on siblings (non-labeled). A major problem with the research on the effects of the gifted label on families is that the research studies reflect *immediate* effects. When there is a public recognition given to one youngster it is reasonable to expect that there is going to be an effect on the family. It is reasonable to expect that the siblings who are not recognized are going to have to make some adjustments to the situation. We don't believe this phenomenon is limited only to the gifted label. Recognition in sports, music, art, or social leadership of any one youngster is bound to have a strong effect on others in the family.

The purpose of the present study is to determine the long-term effects of the gifted label. The population used in this study was families where a youngster had been identified as gifted at least five years previous. While the five year criterion is arbitrary, we feel confident that any effects that were only "immediate" would have been extinguished after five years. Effects from the label after five years were considered indicative of long-term influence.

METHOD

Participants

Participants in this study were youngsters who had been labeled, their siblings, and their parents. Gifted youngsters were those who had been labeled while attending a consolidated junior high school (grades 7–9) serving six rural communities in the Midwest. The students had been identified as gifted based on composite scores on the WISC-R, Iowa Test of Basic Skills (typically upper 10%), grade point average, and parent, teacher, and self-ratings. Each identified student participated in a special program called the Student Talent Program (STP). Of the 67 families who received the research materials, completed forms were returned by N = 53 parents (27 mothers, 26 fathers) (41.7%); N = 28 siblings (f = 12, m = 16) (19%); N = 38 gifted (f = 20, m = 18) (46.9%).

In order to answer the research question regarding long-term effects on families, participants in the study were organized in matched pairs. There were (N = 25) matched pairs of gifted youngsters (M =13; F=12; mean age, 20.0) with their siblings (M = 13; F = 12; mean age, 19.9). Each gifted youngster was matched with each sibling. (Siblings always refers to brothers and sisters not labeled gifted.) There were (N = 44) matched pairs of gifted youngsters with their parents. (Each gifted youngster was matched with each of his or her parents.) And, there were (N = 31) matched pairs of siblings with parents. (Again, each sibling was matched with each of his or her parents.) Thus, the matched pairs consisted of:

a. gifted to siblings
b. gifted to parents
c. siblings to parents

Instrument

Perceptions of Family Communication Scale (PFC). The PFC is a seven-item scale developed to measure family perceptions regarding having had a family member in a special educational program (STP) for students identified as gifted. The PFC is in the initial phases of development and extensive work on validity needs to be completed. The seven questions provide a short and simple measure of the family perception of happiness regarding participation in a gifted program, perception of communication about such participation, and an index of whether or not a family would want a member to participate if they had to do it again.

Procedures

The PFC scale was mailed to all families who had had a member in the Student Talent Program (STP) at least five years ago. The parents, gifted youngsters and siblings completed their own PFC scale and returned them in sealed envelopes. All possible pairs from within each family were used for analysis.

Data Analysis

The PFC scale was analyzed with matched-pairs t-tests (Huck, Cormier, & Bounds, 1974; SPSS Inc., 1986). This procedure was used to account for the logical ties between the scores of the paired respondents (i.e., gifted and their siblings, gifted and their parents, siblings and their parents).

RESULTS

Matched pairs t-tests revealed several differences which were significant at the $p = .05$ level. (See Table 1.) Siblings perceived themselves as significantly happier about the gifted youngster's participation in STP than the gifted youngster perceived their siblings to be ($t = 2.45$, $p = .04$). Siblings compared to gifted perceived their families to have been more open in their communication about the gifted label and participation in STP ($t = 2.04$, $p = .05$). Parents compared to gifted believed more family attention was focused on the gifted youngster because of the selection for STP ($t = 3.77$, $p < .01$). Siblings perceived fathers to be happier about the gifted youngster's participation in STP than the fathers perceived themselves to be ($t = 2.32$, $p = .03$). Lastly, gifted youngsters compared to parents were more positive about participating in STP if they had it to do over again ($t = -2.38$, $p = .02$).

DISCUSSION

One of the most often asked questions by parents regarding the gifted label is "How will the label affect the other siblings?" A review of studies focusing on the effects of the gifted label on family dynamics, especially siblings, provides parents with reason to be concerned. While only a few studies have been published on effects on siblings, the trend is that giftedness does cause adjustment problems for non-identified siblings.

As stated earlier in the article, when one youngster receives public recognition for a positive, it makes good sense to us that such recognition will affect family dynamics. Also, it is almost impossible to deny the common notion that if one child is gifted then non-identified siblings fall into that category known as "nongifted." It is not difficult to imagine the struggles of a youngster who has to overcome the implied label of "nongifted."

Table I   Matched Pairs T-Tests on the Perceptions of Family Communication Scale (PFC)

	N	Mean	Standard Deviation	t	p
Gifted-Siblings Relationship					
Mother's Happiness	17	2.0–1.9	.7–.3	.70	.50
Father's Happiness	16	2.1–1.9	.6–.3	1.46	.16
Siblings' Happiness	10	2.4–2.0	.5–.0	2.45	.04¹
Open Communication	16	2.9–2.6	.6–.7	1.07	.30
Considerable Attention Given	22	3.3–3.0	.6–.6	1.16	.26
Would Participate Again	13	1.6–1.8	.6–.4	1.00	.34
Overall Scale	21	2.6-2.3	.7–.6	2.04	.051
Gifted-Parent Relationship					
Mother's Happiness	35	1.7-1.7	.7–.4	.00	1.00
Father's Happiness	36	1.8-1.8	.8–.4	.00	1.00
Siblings' Happiness	12	2.2-1.9	.9–.3	1.17	.27
Open Communication	29	2.4-2.2	.9–.6	1.24	.23
Considerable Attention Given	35	3.3-2.8	.8–.7	3.77	.001²
Would Participate Again	35	1.7-2.0	.8–.5	− 2.38	.02¹
Overall Scale	34	2.3-2.2	.7–.6	.34	.74
Sibling-Parent Relationship					
Mother's Happiness	23	1.7-1.8	.4–.4	− .62	.54
Father's Happiness	22	1.7-1.9	.4–.2	− 2.32	.31¹
Siblings' Happiness	15	1.9-2.1	.6–.3	− 1.00	.33
Open Communication	18	2.6-2.3	.9–.7	1.00	.33
Considerable Attention Given	20	3.1-2.8	.6–.5	1.42	.17
Would Participate Again	14	1.7-1.9	.5–.3	− 1.38	.19
Overall Scale	21	2.2-2.2	.7–.6	.04	.97

1. $p < .05$
2. $p < .01$

The present research study indicates that the gifted label does not appear to have long-term negative effects for siblings or the family as a whole. Families in this study had at least five years to "get used to" the label and whatever negative initial effects may have been evident, they did not hold. All family members reported overall positive feelings about having had one member identified as gifted and who participated in a special gifted program in school.

Contrary to some of the studies done on families with gifted (e.g., Albert, 1980; Ballering & Koch, 1984; Cornell, 1983), the present study indicates that over time it is the *gifted youngster* who has uneasiness regarding the family. Our findings indicate that gifted youngsters enjoyed participating in a gifted program and clearly would do it again if given the same opportunity. However, these same youngsters did not perceive their siblings as being very positive about the label nor did they perceive the family openly discussing the issue. It is our hypothesis that gifted youngsters are *uneasy* (and perhaps unrealistic) about the effects of the label on family members.

There is a considerable amount of labeling of youngsters in schools for a variety of academic reasons. The effects of labels on youngsters with handicapped learning needs have been widely acknowledged (see Jones, 1972; Rist & Harrell, 1982). There are increasing efforts to label youngsters as gifted yet little research has been done to determine what short-term and long-term effects such procedures have.

Family therapists, school counselors and school psychologists should anticipate immediate difficulties for siblings, and to some extent parents, when a youngster is identified as gifted. But, it seems that in the long-term it is the gifted youngster who needs some attention regarding the label. Gifted youngsters remain somewhat "suspicious" of the feelings and attitudes of siblings and parents regarding their positive label.

Unequivocally, more research is needed on the effects of the gifted label on family dynamics. Such research must include both immediate and long-term effects. There is evidence to believe the effects do change over time. It is our belief that the gifted label will continue to be used by schools on an increasingly wider scale. If such is the case, continued research on the effects of the positive label on family dynamics is imperative.

REFERENCES

Albert, R. S. (1980). Family positions and the attainment of eminence: A study of special family positions and special family experiences. *Gifted Child Quarterly, 24,* 87–95.

Ballering, L. D., & Koch, A. (1984). Family relations when a child is gifted. *Gifted Child Quarterly, 28,* 140–143.

Colangelo, N., & Dettman, D. F. (1985). Families of gifted children. In S. Ehly, J. Conoly, & D. M. Rosenthal (Eds.), *Working with parents of exceptional children.* St. Louis: C. V. Mosby Publishers.

Colangelo, N., & Kelly, K. (1983). A study of student, parent, and teacher attitudes toward gifted programs and gifted students. *Gifted Child Quarterly, 27,* 107–110.

Cornell, D. G. (1983). Gifted children: The impact of positive labeling on the family system. *American Journal of Orthopsychiatry, 53,* 322–335.

Fisher, E. (1981). The effect of labeling on gifted children and their families. *Roeper Review, 3,* 49–51.

Hackney, H. (1981). The gifted child, the family, and the school. *Gifted Child Quarterly, 25,* 51–54.

Hobbs, N. (Ed.). (1975). *The future of children: Categories, labels, and their consequences.* San Francisco: Jossey-Bass.

Huck, S. W., Cormier, W. H., & Bounds, W. G. (1974). *Reading statistics and research.* New York: Harper & Row.

Jones, R. (1972). Labels and stigma in special education. *Exceptional Children, 38,* 553–564.

Marland, S. P. (1972). Education of the gifted and talented: Report to the Congress of the United States by the U.S. Commissioner of Education. Washington, D.C.: U.S. Government Printing Office.

Peterson, D. (1977). The heterogeneously gifted child. *Gifted Child Quarterly, 21*, 396–408.

Rist, R., & Harrell, J. (1982). Labeling the learning disabled child: The social ecology of educational practice. *American Journal of Orthopsychiatry, 52*, 146–160.

Robinson, A. (1986). Brave new directions: Needed research on the labeling of gifted children. *Gifted Child Quarterly, 30*, 11–14.

SPSS Inc. (1986). *SPSSX user's guide, 2nd ed.* New York: McGraw-Hill.

Sunderlin, A. (1981). Gifted children and their siblings. In B. S. Miller & M. Puce (eds.), *The gifted child, the family and the community.* New York: Walter.

Weiss, P., & Gallagher, J. J. (1980). The effects of personal experience on attitudes toward gifted education. *Journal for the Education of the Gifted, 3*, 194–206.

Index

Note: References to tables or figures are indicated by *italic type* and the addition of *"t"* or *"f"* respectively

**CORWIN
PRESS**

The Corwin Press logo—a raven striding across an open book—represents the union of courage and learning. Corwin Press is committed to improving education for all learners by publishing books and other professional development resources for those serving the field of K–12 education. By providing practical, hands-on materials, Corwin Press continues to carry out the promise of its motto: **"Helping Educators Do Their Work Better."**

CPSIA information can be obtained at www.ICGtesting.com
Printed in the USA
BVOW09s1102300616

453953BV00003B/3/P